CONTENTS

INTRODUCTION

The great questions about human life are rarely asked. In a culture dedicated to selfish pursuits, we have little time to ask about origins, values, and destiny. Our concerns deal with *today*. Pragmatic attitudes undermine our sense of values. Ultimate questions seem to go begging.

Our understanding of the nature and purpose of human life has undergone a radical transformation within the past generation. Instead of the sanctity of human life, we speak of its quality. Our morals are controlled by the marketplace and personal rights. Altruism, duty, responsibility, and accountability appear outmoded. The cult of the individual is the religion of the land, and all serious questions about right and wrong are flavored by personal convenience and the pursuit of pleasure.

The quest for personal happiness exceeds our understanding of truth and morality. But such hedonism is a dead-end street, leading nowhere. The self cannot grow when it looks inward. There is no way to control or govern society for good ends when personal needs outweigh our concern for others.

One of the great tragedies of our time is the elimination of a philosophy of life with God at its center, and the subsequent establishment of man as the ultimate objective and greatest concern. God is relegated to religious circles which scarcely influence society. Religion and talk of God are tolerated, but never seriously considered. Our schools have been stripped of religious influence . . . and all in the name of pluralism and the rights of the individual.

He who believes most must now give way to him who believes least. Religious views are held in great suspicion. "How can those ideas be relevant in a scientific age?" we are questioned. Many have no time for God, choosing rather to ignore and neglect his role and importance in their lives.

But what has all this secularism and individualism produced? Is there a greater degree of happiness? Is there less crime? Has our nation been delivered from its psychological troubles? Do our marriages and families reveal the blessings of selfism? Are we closer to peace on earth? Are questions of poverty, alcoholism, drug abuse, pornography, divorce, abortion, venereal disease, diminishing or increasing? Is everything answered by money? Have cheating, stealing, lying, and killing been reduced?

It's time for intellectual honesty and courage. Whatever we're doing, it's not making us better. We seem to be destroying ourselves, all the while searching for something more that we may have missed. What are we looking for? What do we hope to discover by our obsession with pleasure and personal needs? Does God have anything to say about our experiences? Does he exist? Does he care? Is there anything he can do about our dilemmas? Can he make us happy?

Secularism says no. Obviously. God is not included in its vocabulary. Religion says yes; but then it proceeds to confuse us with a multitude of viewpoints about the existence, presence, and involvement of God in this world. Religious brand names seem to struggle for potential proselytes, rather than to proclaim truth to confused minds and offer spiritual food for starving hearts.

But life's greatest questions *are* consistently dealt with in one book. Some call it the "Book of all books"—the best seller of all time, the Bible. Its message is like a breath of fresh air in a polluted atmosphere. It speaks with authority and clarity about human life and its problems. It claims to be the Word of God Himself, given to every generation. It speaks of origins, values, and destiny in simple, easy-to-understand terms. It spends no time proving the existence of God, but begins its message assuming that he exists and that he is active in the affairs of human life. It tells us why we were made, why we are here, and where we are going. It explains history, and does so with an accuracy that most ancient documents lack.

Though not a textbook on science, its statements about the universe and the processes of nature are amazingly accurate, though often described in the language of a particular generation. It is a human book. It does not seek to hide the weaknesses and failures of people. It tells the truth when most would cover it up. It gives hope and encouragement to the most depressed among us, and reassures us all of what to expect in the future. It frequently demands our obedience and emphasizes the importance of faith in the God it so marvelously portrays, a God who is personal, knowable, loving, just, holy, and true.

The great need of society is to return to the pages of the Bible and find the answers to life's greatest and most important questions. If that took place on a large scale, our world could be revolutionized. Individuals could be rescued from drowning in a sea of secularism, hedonism, materialism, and individualism. We could begin again—a fresh start—with new direction that would shape our tomorrows with hope.

Nothing else is working. It's worth a try. Many have found such hope, peace, joy, and love through a personal relationship with the God who made us and through an understanding of the origins, values, and destiny of human life that the Bible presents.

Martin Luther wrote these opening lines in his famous church hymn, "A Mighty Fortress Is Our God":

> A mighty fortress is our God,
> A bulwark never failing;
> Our helper He amid the flood
> Of mortal ills prevailing.

Let's face it—the "mortal ills" of our culture are in great need of a "helper . . . amid the flood." Before we drown, let's take another look at who we are from God's point of view (as taught in the Bible). And then let's ask ourselves: "What difference does it make?"

PART ONE

WHERE DO I COME FROM?

Through His unique creation of man, all that God wished to show of Himself—His perfections, His purity, His love—could be seen and most fully appreciated. For a person to fulfill this function is life. And anything less than this is less than life.

—David C. Needham, *Birthright*

C H A P T E R

1

WHEN
DID IT
ALL BEGIN?

Where did we come from? Many of us wonder. Facts from recorded history and archaeological discovery take us back about 10,000 years—no more! Everything else is just theory.

Textbooks and articles on human life abound. They tell us that men and women first appeared millions of years ago. But the evidence for such reasoning remains questionable. It's just guesswork. It can't be proven.

When did life begin? And how? These questions are important, but not many are asking them. Our obsession with the present drowns out the significance of the past. The word *now* has replaced our interest in *then*.

When pieces of human bone are discovered and declared to be several million years old, we accept the verdict because the information appeared in the local newspaper or was referred to on the evening news. We rarely stop to question. The past just doesn't seem important.

John was a successful businessman, married, with two fine children. But one day he decided to "have an affair." He found he wasn't satisfied with that one experience, so he decided to indulge his libido to its full extent. After years of doing what his sexual desires dictated, he came to me for counsel. It turned out his wife was less than thrilled with his sexual exploits. So were his children.

When I mentioned his accountability to God, he became indignant: "What has God got to do with this?" he replied. "Do you believe in God?" I asked. "No. That's just for children. That's just a helpful religious story—nothing more." He then proceeded to give me a rather erudite lecture on evolution and the fact that we were all once animals. While he wanted help for his marital and family problems, in no way did he want to accept his accountability before God. He saw nothing morally wrong with his life style. He was simply doing what an animal would do!

I tried to persuade him otherwise, but he would not hear of it. At that point, I could offer him no help. He went elsewhere for advice. But his words made me stop and think. Frankly, it does make a difference how human life began. If humans are merely products of biological evolution, then why not act like animals? Why not stop feeling guilty for our actions?

What Does the Bible Teach?

The Bible, in contrast with most viewpoints on the origin of man, is refreshingly simple. It begins by declaring that there is a God. He exists and we can know him. Very little is done to prove the fact. The very first verse of the Bible reads, "In the beginning God created the heavens and the earth." Simple.

After creating the physical and material universe, including earth, the Bible teaches that God created fish, animals, and birds. Then, without much fanfare, Scripture gives this concise report:

> Then God said, "Let us make man in our image, in our likeness, and let them rule over the fish of the sea and the birds of the air, over the livestock, over all the earth, and over all the creatures that move along the ground."
> So God created man in his own image, in the image of God he created him; male and female he created them (Genesis 1:26, 27).

There it is: God created man in his own image. That means that we are somehow like God. We are like we are because he made us like himself.

In the second chapter of Genesis, a few more details are given. In verse 7 we are told:

> And the LORD God formed man from the dust of the ground and breathed into his nostrils the breath of life, and man became a living being.

When, then, did human life begin? It began when God "breathed" into the physical body which he had made out of the elements of the soil. It was the "breath of life" because it came from God himself.

Details about the creation of the woman are quite interesting:

> So the LORD God caused the man to fall into a deep sleep; and while he was sleeping, he took one of the man's ribs and closed up the place with flesh. Then the LORD God made a woman from the rib he had taken out of the man, and he brought her to the man (Genesis 2:21-22).

It's fascinating that God did not take a bone out of man's foot or out of his head—it came out of his side! The principle of companionship was understood from the moment that first woman was created. Male and female, with all their distinct and unique functions and features, were created "in the image of God."

The Breath of Life

Human life began through the creative power of God. Specifically, it comes from his "breath." When God breathed, life began. It was life from God, not simply the air we breathe.

The Hebrew language in which the Old Testament was first written contains a plural form of the word *life* in Genesis 2:7. It was the "breath of *lives*." It seems to indicate more than one kind of life. It certainly means physical life, but it implies more than simple, physical existence.

Genesis 2:9 refers to the "tree of life," and the plural form of *life* is used once again. In Psalm 16:11, King David is talking to God and says, "You have made known to me the path of life." The word *life* is again the plural form. But the use of this plural is most enlightening in Daniel 12:2, when we learn of the future resurrection of believers. It says, "Multitudes who sleep in the dust of the earth will awake: some to everlasting life, others to shame and everlasting contempt." The plural form of the word *life*, combined with the word *everlasting*, is rich with meaning. It includes physical resurrection *and* the immortality of the soul (or personality) of man.

While I don't want to make too much of the plural form of *life*, it becomes important when we consider what happened to Adam when he disobeyed God. In Genesis 2:16-17 we read:

> And the LORD God commanded the man, "You are free to eat from any tree in the garden; but you must not eat from the tree of the knowledge of good and evil, for when you eat of it you will surely die."

We all know the rest of the story: Adam did eat of the tree. But did he die physically that very day? No. He lived for many years after the event. In what sense then, did Adam die the day he ate of the forbidden fruit? If we understand the teaching of the Bible, we would conclude that Adam died spiritually the day he ate of the tree of the knowledge of good and evil. His physical death many years later was simply the consequence of his spiritual death.

Two Kinds of Death?

Physical death is an inevitable fact that all of us must face. People die every day, and no one has been able to avoid it. In Job 34:14-15, one of Job's so-called friends spoke of God's control over life and death:

> If it were his intention and he withdrew his spirit and breath, all mankind would perish together and man would return to the dust.

The New Testament agrees. James 2:26 says that "As the body without the spirit is dead, so faith without deeds is dead." When the spirit or breath of God is removed, physical death occurs. Every one of us is scheduled to face this event. Hebrews 9:27 says, "man is destined to die once, and after that to face judgment." Psalm 104:29 adds, "when you take away their breath, they die and return to the dust."

When God removes the spirit, the body dies. And it's not long afterward that visible evidence of the fact mounts—the body begins to decay. When my father died, I wanted people to understand that the body they saw in the casket at the funeral was not the spirit or soul. I put a sign on the inside lid of the casket which read, "Away from the body . . . at home with the Lord" (words from 2 Corinthians 5:8). Physical death is the separation of the body from the soul and the spirit of man.

But the Bible also speaks of another kind of death— spiritual death. People can be physically alive, but spiritually dead. That's how Ephesians 2:1 characterizes the lives of a group of believers before they became Christians: "you were dead in your transgressions and sins." Sin is the cause of spiritual *and* physical death. In Romans 5:12 we read:

> Therefore, just as sin entered the world through one man, and death through sin, . . . in this way death came to all men, because all sinned.

Even before people had received any standard of what was right and wrong, people died. Verse 14 of that same chapter says:

> Nevertheless, death reigned from the time of Adam to the time of Moses, even over those who did not sin by breaking a command, as did Adam, who was a pattern of the one to come.

The law given to Moses contains God's standards of right and wrong. But before that time, people still died even though their sin was not the same as Adam's. Death was a fact, and everybody experienced it (and they still do!).

Two kinds of life were given to men and women—physical and spiritual. And because of sin, two kinds of death are experienced—physical and spiritual. The two kinds of life resulted from God's breathing into man's nostrils his own breath or spirit. God is called "the Father of our spirits" (Hebrews 12:9), and the "God of the spirits of all mankind" (Numbers 16:22; 27:16).

What about the Soul?

We have learned so far that God created man's body from the dust of the ground, and that he imparted two kinds of life—physical and spiritual—when he breathed his spirit into man's nostrils. By this act, God created "a living being," or a "living soul."

The soul is the personhood of human life. It stands often in the Bible in contrast to the body or flesh. It has many characteristics that indicate mental activity. It expresses various emotions. Job 30:25 says, "Has not my soul grieved for the poor?" David said in Psalm 42:1, "my soul pants for you, O God," and in verse 2, "my soul thirsts for God, for the living God." In Psalm 62:1 we read, "My soul finds rest in God alone." David also writes, "Be at rest once more, O my soul, for the LORD has been good to you" (Psalm 116:7). According to Song of Solomon 1:7, the soul "loves" (NASB). In Ezekiel 18:4 we read:

> For every living soul belongs to me, the father as well as the son—both alike belong to me. The soul who sins is the one who will die.

Verse 20 in that same chapter says, "the soul who sins is the one who will die." The soul or person is capable of sinning and therefore dying. According to Hebrews 10:39 (NASB), our faith in God and his work in our behalf can lead to the "preserving [or saving] of the soul." Psalm 49:15 expresses the confidence of one whose trust is in the Lord: "But God will redeem my soul from the grave." The soul can be saved and redeemed.

Our English word *psychology* comes from a Greek term used in the New Testament for *soul*. Psychology is the study of the soul or personality of man. This word occurs over 900 times in the Septuagint, a Greek translation of the Old Testament.

The New Testament uses the word *soul* 101 times, and makes it interchangeable with our English word *person*. The soul loves, hates, thinks, perceives, and decides. The word *soul* can be used of people in a group who are being counted (Acts 27:37; 1 Peter 3:20).

Is the Spirit the Same As the Soul?

Since both *spirit* and *soul* involve the immaterial, invisible part of man, it is easy to make them identical. Some people believe that human life is composed of two parts: body and soul, or physical and psychological (or spiritual). But before we make a judgment on this, we should consider the Bible's teaching in 1 Thessalonians 5:23:

> May God himself, the God of peace, sanctify you through and through. May your whole spirit, soul and body be kept blameless at the coming of our Lord Jesus Christ.

Some believe that man is composed of body, soul, and spirit. Man is physical, psychological, and spiritual. The physical makes him aware of the material world and the people around him; the psychological makes him aware of himself (self-consciousness); and the spiritual makes him aware of God.

The apostle Paul makes a further distinction between the soul and the spirit in 1 Corinthians 15:44:

> It is sown a natural body, it is raised a spiritual body. If there is a natural body, there is also a spiritual body.

Our bodies now are called "natural bodies," or bodies characterized primarily by the soul or personality of man. In the future, when our bodies are resurrected, the primary characteristic or controlling factor will be the spirit.

Hebrews 4:12 also distinguishes between the soul and the spirit of man:

> The word of God is living and active. Sharper than any double-edged sword, it penetrates even to dividing soul and spirit, joints and marrow; it judges the thoughts and attitudes of the heart.

The Bible has the power to penetrate to that point which separates the soul from the spirit; and it can work on both. Even though we cannot fully understand this distinction, the Bible is able to impact both parts.

What Is an Image?

It is one thing to say that we are made in the "image of God," but it is quite another to understand what that means. Since God did not have a physical body when he created human life, the *image* cannot refer to our mortal bodies. So to what does it refer?

The "image" of something reflects a certain similarity or likeness. Coins show the image of past presidents of our country. The United States dollar bill features the image of George Washington. The word *image* can refer to a painting, statue, or printed figure. In Greek thought, an image is closely related to the reality of what it represents. The essence or nature of the thing appears in the image.

When Jesus asked the Pharisees and Herodians of his day "Whose portrait [image] is this? And whose inscription?" he was referring to a Roman coin called a "denarius" (Matthew 22:15-22). On the coin was the likeness or image of Caesar. In that case, the likeness or image is merely the appearance of a person.

Jesus is called "the image of the invisible God" (Colossians 1:15). In Christ, we clearly see God himself. Hebrews 1:3 says that Jesus is "the exact representation of his [God's] being." Jesus is more than a mere appearance or likeness of God. He is himself God in human flesh. Romans 8:29 tells us:

> For those God foreknew he also predestined to be conformed to the likeness of His Son, that he might be the firstborn among many brothers.

One of God's great plans for believers is to conform them to the image of his Son. We are going to be "like him, for we shall see him as he is" (1 John 3:2). Christ is called "the image of God" (2 Corinthians 4:4), and we who are believers are constantly developing into His image. Consider 2 Corinthians 3:18:

And we, who with unveiled faces all reflect the
Lord's glory, are being transformed into his likeness with ever-increasing glory, which comes
from the Lord, who is the Spirit.

A process of transformation is going on inside the believer that causes us to reflect the "image" of Jesus Christ
himself! That is not talking about a physical likeness. It
must deal with our immaterial part—the soul. Something
is happening to our attitudes and emotions, to our reac-
tions toward people. Our personality is changing and start-
ing to reflect the beauty of Jesus Christ. We begin to do
what he would say and do if he were here. This process will
be completed one day when Jesus comes again. Then we
will "bear the likeness of the man from heaven" (1 Corinthians 15:49), just as we have "borne the likeness of the
earthly man."

It is marvelous indeed that we were made in the image
and likeness of God. Immediate self-worth and dignity are
thereby given to us. There is something about human beings that reflects the divine.

One of the amazing facts of Scripture concerning the
image of God is given in Genesis 5:1-3, where we learn
about the children of Adam and Eve:

This is the written account of Adam's line.
When God created man, he made him in the
likeness of God. He created them male and
female; at the time they were created, he blessed
them and called them "man."
When Adam had lived 130 years, he had a son
in his own likeness, in his own image; and he named
him Seth.

A few theologians have spoken of man's losing the
image of God through his sin and fall. The image is often
thought of as "marred" by sin and the fall of Adam. But
these verses in Genesis 5, written after the fall of Adam,
seem to indicate otherwise. Lewis Sperry Chafer believed
as much when he wrote, "unregenerate, fallen man bears
the image of his Creator."[1]

WHERE DO I COME FROM?

The Bible maintains that every male and female born into this world has been made or designed in the image of God and after his likeness, and that this does not refer to the physical body but to the immaterial part of man—the soul.

In What Sense Are We Like God?

We all know (with great embarrassment at times!) that we are like our parents; but in what sense are we "after the likeness" of God?

In a marvelous discussion of the question, What is man? in the book, *Christianity on Trial*, Colin Chapman writes:

> To say that man is like God means that: Just as God is personal, so man is personal. Just as God has mind and can think and communicate, so man has a mind and can think and communicate; he is rational. Just as God has will and can decide and make free choices, so man has a will and can make certain free choices; he is responsible and accountable. Just as God has emotions and can feel, so man has emotions and can feel.[2]

It is in the realm of the soul that we see that likeness to God. Though we are like him, we are not the same as he is. He is not limited by space, time, body, knowledge, or power. But he is personal and knowable, and we are made in his image and after his likeness. That's the foundation of all self-worth and human dignity.

I once became particularly frustrated when I tried to explain this to a teenage girl. She had so many reasons not to believe what I was saying. She couldn't see that the only thing that could rescue her from the pit of despair and defeat that dominated her thinking, the only thing that could save her from a contemplated suicide, was the knowledge that she was created in the image of God and after his likeness. No matter how abused she'd been in life, no matter how many times she'd been rejected by parents and friends, the truth of the Bible still stood—she was made in the image of God!

After several talks, the light of that truth began to capture her interest. Slowly she became convinced that she was something wonderful because of it. She was made and designed by the eternal God who loved her. Today she is a growing, loving person because of what she learned about the origin of human life. Hope is often rooted in our understanding of creation.

Colin Chapman has summarized three theories of human life:[3]

1. Man is a creature created in the image of God—the God of the Bible.
   (The view of biblical Christianity)
2. Man is a creature created by God—but not the God of the Bible.
   (The view of primal religion, Islam, and deism)
3. Man is not the creation of God because there is no personal creator.
   (The view of humanism, existentialism, communism, and eastern religions)

Modern Judaism certainly teaches that man is created by God, but it denies Christian beliefs about the origin and presence of a sinful nature. Islam argues much for the dignity of man as God's creation, but sees little similarity between God and man except for the fact that God brought man into existence.

Biblical Christianity understands human life as created by God, in his image and after his likeness. We are like God in that we have similar mental, emotional, and volitional responses. We are unlike God in that we are limited by the needs and functions of our bodies. He is eternal; we are not. He is infinite; we are finite. He is everywhere at once; we are limited by space and time. He can do anything; we obviously can't. He knows everything; we wish we did! He has no sin nature and never sins; we do, and so did our parents.

Origins affect values and destiny. It's hard to discuss the meaning of life until we settle on how it all began. The beauty of being created in the image of God and after his likeness must precede all discussion about the nature and purpose of human life. If we are not clear here, everything else will be distorted, and the results will be devastating.

The comments of George Sweeting provide a good conclusion to this first chapter:

> The philosopher would say that the proper study of mankind is man himself. That may be good philosophy, but it is poor theology. The Bible tells us that man cannot be understood in himself, but only in and through his relationship to God. Only in the light of man's relationship to God can he see himself as he really is. He is not God, but man, with God-given powers and responsibilities. In his ability to reason, in his will, in his conscience, man is made in the image of God.[4]

---

1. Lewis Sperry Chafer, *Systematic Theology*, vol. 2 (Dallas, Tex.: Dallas Seminary Press, 1947), p. 167.

2. Colin Chapman, *Christianity on Trial* (Wheaton: Tyndale House Publishers, Inc., 1975), p. 220.

3. Chapman, *Christianity on Trial*, pp. 217-311.

4. George Sweeting, "What Is Man?" *Moody Monthly*, June 1979, pp. 30-31.

C H A P T E R

2

WHAT WENT WRONG?

While sitting around the table enjoying a meal with the family several years ago, one of my children blurted out, "Daddy, where did sin come from?" I was tempted to say, "Ask your mother!" But I knew that wouldn't work, so I made an attempt to answer this young, inquisitive mind.

What I thought would be easy turned out to be much more difficult than I had imagined. When I said, "From what Adam did," my child answered, "Why?" (Why do kids always ask why?) Every time I attempted an explanation, I kept getting that reply—"Why?"

Although I became a little frustrated that day with the kind of questions kids can ask, I was reminded of what all of us face from time to time. There are many questions and too few answers. One of the most troublesome questions deals with what sin is and where it came from. How did it happen? Who did it first? Why did God allow sin in the first place? Why are we sinners because of what Adam did? What is sin anyway? What causes us to sin?

The questions go on. They need to be answered, because they deal profoundly with who we are and why we do what we do. And there is no lack of variety in the way the questions are answered. Some people see it as a strictly religious matter, something that religion has made up to keep people in line. Today's secular mind has denied the reality of sin, even though it's obvious that people do evil things in this world. But denying sin will not help to solve the problems of evil and crime.

Did God Create Sin?

If God created everything, does that include sin? Some people think so, but the Bible denies it. Several years ago I was confronted by a man who was teaching a Bible study in the home of some friends. He taught that God created sin, and he used a verse in the Bible to "prove" it. He referred to Isaiah 45:7, which says (in the old King James Version) that God creates evil. The New American Standard Version of that verse reads:

> The One forming light and creating darkness, causing well-being and creating *calamity*; I am the LORD who does all these.

The verse does not teach that God creates evil or sin, but that he brings judgment or calamity upon those who do.

The Bible emphatically declares that God cannot sin and that he never tempts any one of us to do evil. First John 1:5 says:

> This is the message we have heard from him and declare to you: God is light; in him there is *no darkness at all.*

James agreed with this when he wrote, "When tempted, no one should say, 'God is tempting me.' For God cannot be tempted by evil, nor does he tempt anyone" (James 1:13).

Jesus never sinned (2 Corinthians 5:21), even though he was "tempted in every way, just as we are" (Hebrews 4:15). Hebrews 6:18 says that "it is impossible for God to lie." God cannot sin, he does not cause it, nor does he tempt anyone to do it.

Was Adam Sinful in the Beginning?

If God neither created sin nor can sin, did he create man with a sinful nature? Once again the Bible is quite clear. Romans 5:12 says:

> Therefore, just as sin entered the world through one man, and death through sin, and in this way death came to all men, because all sinned. . . .

Sin entered the world through the act of Adam, although sin obviously existed before Adam. Verse 19 of that same chapter says, "through the disobedience of the one man the many were made sinners." The Bible focuses on Adam's disobedience when describing the reality of sin in the world. Before Adam disobeyed, sin was not "in the world," though it existed.

Man was morally good when God created him: "This only have I found: God made mankind upright, but men have gone in search of many schemes" (Ecclesiastes 7:29). Genesis 1:31 calls everything that God created "very good."

When God made man, he made him with a pure and good nature. But Adam had no moral *character* at that point—moral character is developed by moral experience. And since Adam had no moral experience when he was created, he did not then have a holy character. He did have a nature that was not sinful, though it was capable of committing sin. Adam had an inherent tendency to do good, but also had the power to choose evil.

How Did Sin Enter the World?

If God did not create sin or cause it, how did it get here in the first place? Genesis 3 tells the story.

Man was placed into a perfect environment in Eden. It was a beautiful garden where man could enjoy the life God had given him and where he could have intimate fellowship with his wonderful Creator. But the scene quickly changed as Adam brought tragedy on himself when he deliberately disobeyed his God.

A strange creature appears in Genesis 3:1 that the Bible describes as a serpent "more crafty than any of the wild animals the LORD God had made." The serpent talks . . . and Eve, Adam's wife, listens. His influence, direct and very persuasive, is immediately felt. According to one commentator:

> It is a feature of the story which should not be neglected that temptation comes to the woman from without—from the serpent; which, whether taken literally or symbolically, represents here a

power of evil suggestion other than man's own thoughts.[1]

The serpent's suggestions and questionings throughout the story indicate that he is the instigator of this whole affair. Notice carefully his approach.

Verse 1—he questions God's commands by implying more than what God had said.

Verse 4—he contradicts the plain statement of God.

Verse 5—he suggests that God's motives are not good and that God's pride keeps him from allowing man to be like him.

Who is this serpent? The Bible leaves no doubt about it. The apostle Paul wrote:

But I am afraid that just as Eve was deceived by the serpent's cunning, your minds may somehow be led astray from your sincere and pure devotion to Christ (2 Corinthians 11:3).

Later in that chapter we read,

And no wonder, for Satan himself masquerades as an angel of light (v. 14).

An even stronger identification of the serpent is found in Revelation 12:9:

The great dragon was hurled down—that ancient serpent called the devil or Satan, who leads the whole world astray. He was hurled to the earth, and his angels with him.

Verse 10 adds that he is called "the accuser of our brothers." Yes, the serpent is none other than Satan, the devil, the powerful but limited archenemy of God.

The Scriptures consistently point a finger at Satan as the cause of sin and the channel through which it came into our world. It is interesting to note that God does not ask the serpent to defend himself when Adam and Eve tried to pass the blame.

It is no more said here, "Wherefore has thou done this?" although the serpent is previously introduced as speaking, and, therefore, as capable of maintaining conversation. Therein lies the supposition that the trial has now reached the fountain-head of sin, the purely evil purpose (the demoniacal) having no deeper ground, and requiring no further investigation.[2]

Satan is guilty. Through his temptation, sin entered the world. This does not relieve Adam and Eve of their responsibility, however, for God's instructions were quite clear. Eve was deceived, according to 1 Timothy 2:14, but Adam deliberately disobeyed (Romans 5:19).

When Did Satan Sin?

Jesus said that Satan was a "murderer from the beginning" (John 8:44). He also called him "a liar and the father of lies." First John 3:8 says, "the devil has been sinning from the beginning."

Before the fall of Adam and Eve, Satan and those angels who followed him fell themselves. Isaiah 14:12-14 gives the details:

How you have fallen from heaven, O morning star, son of the dawn! You have been cast down to the earth, you who once laid low the nations! You said in your heart, "I will ascend to heaven; I will raise my throne above the stars of God; I will sit enthroned on the mount of assembly, on the utmost heights of the sacred mountain. I will ascend above the tops of the clouds; I will make myself like the Most High."

There has been some question as to whether this is a direct reference to Satan. In verse 4 we learn that these words were spoken concerning "the king of Babylon." At the end of the chapter (vv. 22-23), it is clear that this is a prophecy concerning the destruction of Babylon. In fact, the whole discussion dealing with Babylon begins in chapter 13 and continues until chapter 14, verse 23.

The problem is that there are things said here about the king of Babylon that could apply only to Satan. The king seems to be a representative figure of the attitude of Satan himself. The statement about his fall from heaven reminds us of what Jesus said in Luke 10:18: "I saw Satan fall like lightning from heaven." Also, the prideful remarks about ascending to heaven, about raising his throne above the stars of God, and being like the Most High God seem more appropriately applied to Satan than to an ancient, earthly king of Babylon.

Another possible connection to the original fall of Satan can be found in Ezekiel 28:11-19. These words (like Isaiah 14) have a historical reference to the king of Tyre; but what is said makes us apply this prophecy to Satan as well. Verses 12-15 suggest the devil's original moral perfection and great beauty.

> " 'You were the model of perfection, full of wisdom and perfect in beauty. You were in Eden, the garden of God; every precious stone adorned you: ruby, topaz and emerald, chrysolite, onyx and jasper, sapphire, turquoise and beryl. Your settings and mountings were made of gold; on the day you were created they were prepared. You were anointed as a guardian cherub, for so I ordained you. You were on the holy mount of God; you walked among the fiery stones. You were blameless in your ways from the day you were created.' "

Can this refer only to the ancient king of Tyre? That seems hard to believe. How was the king of Tyre "in Eden, the garden of God"? Can we say that the king of Tyre was "perfect" and "blameless"? Was the king of Tyre "the anointed cherub"? Hardly. The passage has a double reference, as do many of the prophecies of the Old Testament. It is a clear statement about the original condition of Satan and testifies that he was created by God previous to the events of Genesis 3.

But something happened to spoil this delightful creature. Ezekiel goes on to say that "wickedness was found" in Lucifer, and he sinned. Verse 17 continues, "Your heart became proud on account of your beauty, and you corrupted your wisdom because of your splendor."

The origin of sin is to be found in the heart of Satan, not God. God created him, but like Adam and Eve, he had the power to choose. His pride was his downfall. His bitterness and hatred of God continue to this day. Though he must know the Bible's teaching concerning his destiny (the lake of fire—hell), he continues his evil ways and stubborn resistance to God and all his purposes.

Lewis Sperry Chafer writes concerning this fall of Satan:

> The ambition to become "like the Most High" was the original sin of this great angel, and no little meaning is attached to the fact that he brought his own identical sin of independence of God as a temptation to Adam and Eve, and that they adopted this philosophy of life.[3]

Satan sought to ruin the "very good" creation of God by destroying the man whom God created in his own image. Though Adam and Eve voluntarily sinned against God, this disobedience came from an outside source and in a very tempting package.

How Did Satan Tempt Adam and Eve?

The Bible speaks of Satan's "cunning" (2 Corinthians 11:3; Genesis 3:1) and reminds us of his schemes (Ephesians 6:11). Satan began by throwing doubt on God's word. He suggested that God did not mean what he had said. He then substituted his word for God's word. Eve went right along with the deception when she added to God's Word (Genesis 3:3), "You must not eat fruit from the tree . . . and you *must not touch it* . . ."

The real bait came when Satan proposed three things:

1. "your eyes will be opened"
2. "you will be like God" (Satan's original desire)
3. "you will know good and evil"

The motivation for disobedience was not appetite, as some suggest, but rather the ambition to be like God. The temptation suggests (as it always does) that they would no longer need the leadership and direction of God in their lives.

The details of Eve's downfall are graphically portrayed in Genesis 3:6:

> When the woman saw that the fruit of the tree was good for food and pleasing to the eye, and also desirable for gaining wisdom, she took some and ate it. She also gave some to her husband, who was with her, and he ate it.

The woman "saw," then "took," and finally "ate." She then persuaded her husband. Adam knew better. He deliberately disobeyed God and went along with Eve. The story has a familiar ring to it! The heart of the temptation is found in what Eve "saw." She saw three things:

1. "the tree was good for food"
2. it was "pleasing to the eye"
3. the tree was "desirable for gaining wisdom"

Some writers like to connect these three statements with the words of 1 John 2:16:

> For everything in the world—the cravings of sinful man, the lust of his eyes and the boasting of what he has and does—comes not from the Father but from the world.

Many of life's temptations are first presented as something "good" for us, rather than the evil that they are. Our natural inclination is to view them as desirable. They seem "delightful." We like to look at them—and in that continual looking and longing are found the seeds of disaster. We are attracted by the knowledge and experience we might receive by giving in to the temptation.

Was the Temptation a Sin?

Life is filled with temptation. If it was sin to be tempted, then most of us would live perpetually in sin with little hope of victory. But the sin of Adam and Eve was not that an evil opportunity presented itself to them. The sin came when "she took some and ate it. She also gave some to her husband, who was with her, and he ate it." It was the eating of the fruit that violated God's specific command:

> You are free to eat from any tree in the garden;
> but you must not eat from the tree of the knowl-
> edge of good and evil, for when you eat of it you
> will surely die (Genesis 2:16-17).

It was no sin to be tempted or even to look at that tree. The sin occurred the moment they ate. Sin is lawlessness, it is the violation of God's commands (1 John 3:4). It is disobedience to the revealed will of God. James 1:14-15 explains the process:

> but each one is tempted when, by his own evil
> desire, he is dragged away and enticed. Then,
> after desire has conceived, it gives birth to sin;
> and sin, when it is full-grown, gives birth to
> death.

Sin is not in the temptation. Otherwise, Jesus would be a sinner, for he was tempted as we are. We cannot blame the temptation or the environment in which it took place. The problem lies in our "own lust." When you seek to satisfy your desires in opposition to God's Word, you sin against God. (The consequences of sin will be discussed in chapter 5.)

The problem of sin and temptation was vividly demonstrated to me one night as I was teaching in a home Bible study. About fifteen people were in the living room of that home, among whom were several new believers and a couple who were not yet Christians. We were studying the Sermon on the Mount, and we came to Matthew 5:27-28:

> You have heard that it was said, "Do not commit
> adultery." But I tell you that anyone who looks at
> a woman lustfully has already committed adul-
> tery with her in his heart.

WHERE DO I COME FROM?

A young man in the group who had just become a Christian jumped to his feet and said, "That does it. I quit! If you expect me to stop looking at other women, you're crazy! It's impossible!" We all persuaded him to stay, and after calming him down I began to explain what I thought Jesus was teaching. I listed several points:

1. It is a sin to commit adultery.
2. The desire to commit adultery is sinful, even though there was no penalty in the law of Moses for mere desire.
3. The word *looks* is in the present tense in the original language, and indicates or implies a habit of life.
4. The word *woman* is singular, not plural. It implies that the lust is concentrating on a particular woman, not women in general.
5. The "lust" does not refer to admiring the physical beauty or assets of the woman, but is the desire to actually commit adultery.
6. What we think about often becomes what we do in a moment of provocation and opportunity. Our thoughts need to be controlled.
7. Sinful desires in the heart (which we all have) will be easily carried out unless we walk in obedience to God's word under the control of the Holy Spirit (Psalm 119:9; Galatians 5:16).

Though that young man had more questions, he began to see the importance of what Jesus said. It is true that we have sinful desires that easily respond to the temptations around us. But admiring a beautiful, sexually attractive woman is not the sin. The sin is desiring to commit adultery. Failure to control that desire can lead to direct disobedience of God's law.

The Nature and Extent of Sin

Sin is not only an *act* of disobedience to God's law; it is equally a *condition* of the heart. Our minds, emotions, and decisions are all affected by sin in our lives. Though the body is not sinful in itself, sin has tremendous effects upon

34

it. The prophet Jeremiah lamented that condition when he wrote,

> The heart is deceitful above all things and beyond cure. Who can understand it? (Jeremiah 17:9).

It's a good question: Who *can* understand the human heart? The prophet knew the answer—only God can. We cannot imagine the depth of depravity and deceit in our own hearts. We don't like to think about it. We often paint ourselves to be good and our motives pure. But we deceive ourselves.

The apostle Paul wrote in Romans 7:14, "I am unspiritual, sold as a slave to sin." He continued later in that letter:

> the sinful mind is hostile to God. It does not submit to God's law, nor can it do so (Romans 8:7).

"I know that nothing good lives in me, that is, in my sinful nature," the great apostle wrote, declaring in 7:17, 20, and 23 that sin was dwelling in him. Whether we like it or not, sin lives in the human heart. No one escapes its corrupting influence or its destructive effects. Isaiah 53:6 says that "We all, like sheep, have gone astray." Proverbs 20:9 adds, "Who can say, 'I have kept my heart pure; I am clean and without sin?'" The answer is obvious. No one can.

John the apostle reminds us that "If we claim to be without sin, we deceive ourselves and the truth is not in us" (1 John 1:8). Verse 10 adds, "If we claim we have not sinned, we make him out to be a liar and his word has no place in our lives."

Why Did God Allow Sin to Exist?

So we are in a predicament. Sin not only surrounds us, it's in us. And that brings up another question: If God is so good, why did he allow sin to take place at all? Admittedly, this is a difficult question and must be approached with some caution. The finite must not presume to understand the infinite. The question centers on two problems: Either God could not prevent sin from happening, or he chose not to do so.

WHERE DO I COME FROM?

There seem to be two options in explaining whether God could prevent sin. We can see God as limited or finite (which the Bible clearly indicates he is not); or that he limited himself by creating man with the power to choose, thereby allowing man to do evil. Since God will ultimately stop man from ever sinning again and will completely remove sin from his eternal city (Revelation 21:27), we must conclude that the second option is the right one: God chose not to prevent man (or the devil) from sinning.

Why would God make such a decision? Did he refuse to prevent sin because sin is a good in itself? No, that is unthinkable. Then did he choose that route because He saw it as a necessary way to accomplish the greatest good? Did he, perhaps, decide that allowing sin to exist brings less evil than preventing it from occurring?

One thing is for sure—he has permitted sin to exist, and since he has permitted it, it must have been right for him to do so. Abraham, the great patriarch of Israel, thought as much when he said, "Will not the Judge of all the earth do right?" (Genesis 18:25). Of course.

Some insist that man would have had no knowledge of good and evil without experiencing sin. But that cannot be true. We know what good and evil are by simply believing what God tells us. We don't have to experience sin to know what it is. If God says that something is sinful, we should believe it. Our personal experience in the matter is irrelevant.

Although we cannot know for certain those purposes of God that are not revealed to us in his written word, we can assume or deduce some things from what he has told us. Adam was created with a holy nature and with a will to choose. God tested him so that through moral experience he might develop a holy character. This is still God's way of producing a holy character. James 1:12 says:

> Blessed is the man who perseveres under trial, because when he has stood the test, he will receive the crown of life that God has promised to those who love him.

Peter said much the same thing when he wrote,

> In this you greatly rejoice, though now for a little while you may have had to suffer grief in all kinds of trials. These have come so that your faith—of greater worth than gold, which perishes even though refined by fire—may be proved genuine and may result in praise, glory and honor when Jesus Christ is revealed (1 Peter 1:6-7).

Hebrews 12:10-11 demonstrates clearly the purpose of God in developing a holy character:

> Our fathers disciplined us for a little while as they thought best; but God disciplines us for our good, that we may share in his holiness. No discipline seems pleasant at the time, but painful. Later on, however, it produces a harvest of righteousness and peace for those who have been trained by it.

A holy character, Peter says, is produced through the trials and discipline of life (1 Peter 1:6, 7, 14-16).

Through his grace, forgiveness, and judgment, God can take the sin of man and reveal his divine character and nature and so bring glory to himself. That is precisely what the Lord did in Egypt with a wicked pharaoh: "I raised you up for this very purpose, that I might display my power in you and that my name might be proclaimed in all the earth" (Romans 9:17). Joseph had a similar experience when his brothers sold him into slavery. Years later, when he had become the second most powerful man in Egypt, he told his fearful brothers that "You intended to harm me, but God intended it for good to accomplish what is now being done, the saving of many lives" (Genesis 50:20).

God can take the sin of man and bring glory to himself. When he judges sin, he proves that he is just and righteous. When he forgives sin, he demonstrates his love and grace. The presence of sin in the world has done much to exalt and glorify the character and attributes of God.

But to those who might say, "Let us do evil that good may result," Paul says, "Their condemnation is deserved"

(Romans 3:8). Those who truly love God will love to please him, just as a happily married couple delights in pleasing each other.

Sin is with us, true. But so is God.

And which is the stronger?

1. James Orr, *God's Image in Man* (Grand Rapids: Wm. B. Eerdmans Publishing Co., 1948), p. 219.

2. John Peter Lange, *Commentary on the Holy Scriptures* (Grand Rapids: Zondervan Publishing House), p. 232.

3. Lewis Sperry Chafer, *Systematic Theology*, vol. 2 (Dallas, Tex.: Dallas Seminary Press, 1947), p. 210.

3

WHY MARRIAGE?

Doesn't everyone know about the birds and the bees? Do we really need another dissertation on sex and marriage? There are so many books on the subject already; it seems that there will be no end to the making of them!

But do we fully understand the origin and purpose of sex and marriage? Many sexual problems crop up because sexual understanding is limited or twisted. We grow up with wrong attitudes and viewpoints, thinking all along that we know all there is to know. We carry these wrong opinions into adult life—and the result is often tragedy, heartache, and great disappointment.

Several years ago a young wife, married only six months, came into my office for marital counseling. Her failure to have a satisfying sexual life with her husband upset her greatly. As far as she was concerned, marital sex was not all that great. In spite of attending premarital classes that had dealt with sexual understanding, she just could not comprehend why sex was so important, for in her experience it was not very satisfying.

She came into that marriage with great expectations and high romantic ideals. It turned out different from what she expected. It was very platonic and unrewarding. She wondered if other people went through the same thing but were afraid to admit it.

Her opinions that day were woefully inadequate, falling far short of biblical ideals and principles. So we started over at the beginning and reviewed the Bible's teaching about sex and marriage.

That wife's experience could be repeated many times over. For years I have conducted marriage seminars in various cities and have received questions, comments, and viewpoints from hundreds of people, both Christians and non-Christians. This has clearly shown that we need to understand the Bible's view of sex and marriage. All of us need to review these principles, even if we have heard them before!

It's like what one husband and wife told me: "After thirty-eight years of marriage, we are finally understanding what the Bible teaches about sex. How foolish, stubborn, and selfish we have been all these years! It's a wonder that we are still married!"

Who Invented Sex?

Who invented sex? Certainly not Playboy magazine! The Bible says that God invented it. He placed within our hearts the desire for sexual involvement and pleasure. It was something beautiful, not dirty. It was good, not bad.

When God created the woman by taking a rib from man, he brought her to the man (Genesis 2:22). God made the first introduction. The man was immediately impressed with the obvious physical resemblance and relationship he had with this woman. He said,

> This is now bone of my bones and flesh of my flesh; she shall be called 'woman,' for she was taken out of man (Genesis 2:23).

Adam understood from the beginning that the woman was an integral part of himself. But even before the man had a chance to grasp what this meant for the future, God gave him the basic principles of sex and marriage:

> For this reason a man will leave his father and mother and be united to his wife, and they will become one flesh (Genesis 2:24).

It would be hard to conceive of a better statement on sex and marriage. Adam might well have said, "What's a father and a mother?" His knowledge at that point was certainly limited. He was totally dependent upon God for what to believe, think, and do. This simple statement establishes three principles about sex, marriage, and the family:

1. How a family is established.
2. How a marriage is determined.
3. How sexual experience is to be conducted.

How a Family Is Established

What a family is and how it should operate will be discussed more thoroughly in chapter 4. But for now we simply want to understand this: Genesis 2:24 reveals . . .

1. A family is composed of a father and a mother.
2. To be a father or a mother necessitates a child.
3. The man establishes the family unit the moment he takes a wife.
4. The man's relationship with his own parents is severed (in some sense) the moment he gets married.

This biblical pattern is often referred to as the "traditional view" or the "nuclear family." Many are out today to redefine the traditional family. Can a family be something besides a father, mother, and child? I'll say more about this in the next chapter.

How a Marriage Is Determined

Genesis 2:24 reveals what it means to be married. God was the original witness to the first marriage. It was he who "performed the ceremony" and he who gave instructions on what should be done. Some things about marriage are obvious:

1. A *marriage involves a man and a woman*. In the words of Jesus Christ, "Haven't you read . . . that at the beginning the Creator 'made them male and female'?" (Matthew 19:4). The words translated *male* and *female* describe the unique

physical features of man and woman that clearly show their differences. They reveal sexual differences and emphasize that God's original design involved "difference," not "sameness." In a day when men often act or look like women and women often act or look like men, it is important to remember God's intention.

Romans 1:26-27 condemns in no uncertain terms the attempt to change God's order:

> Because of this, God gave them over to shameful lusts. Even their women exchanged natural relations for unnatural ones. In the same way the men also abandoned natural relations with women and were inflamed with lust for one another. Men committed indecent acts with other men, and received in themselves the due penalty for their perversion.

The term *indecent acts* suggests something which lacks shape or design. Homosexual behavior violates God's original purpose for sex and marriage. It is "natural" for a man to be attracted sexually to a woman; but it is "unnatural" to be attracted to the same sex.

God's attitude toward those who attempt to reverse or eliminate the distinctive roles of male and female is clear from Deuteronomy 22:5:

> A woman must not wear men's clothing, nor a man wear women's clothing, for the LORD your God detests anyone who does this.

2. A *marriage is an interdependent relationship between a man and a woman.* Concepts of independence, frequently promoted in today's culture, are not taught in the Bible. The apostle Paul wrote in 1 Corinthians 11:8-9:

> For man did not come from woman, but woman from man; neither was man created for woman, but woman for man.

This was true for Adam and Eve; but from then on, another principle applies. Paul continues in verses 11-12 of the same chapter:

In the Lord, however, woman is not independent
of man, nor is man independent of woman. For
as woman came from man, so also man is born
of woman. But everything comes from God.

Eve was taken and formed from a part of Adam's body,
and men are born out of the womb of a woman. God uses
this to show our dependency upon our marital partners. We
are uniquely related to each other and must understand
our mutual dependence upon one another. When we forget
or ignore this, marriage becomes something less than God
intended. A sense of dependency upon the marital partner
is part of what constitutes a marriage.

3. *A marriage is an intimate companionship between a man and
a woman.* Genesis 2:18 makes it crystal clear that the basic
purpose of marriage is companionship, not merely human
reproduction. Having children makes a family; but it does
not necessarily make a marriage. Adam's need for companionship became distressingly obvious when God told
him to name all the animals. Adam did so, one by one, until
all the beasts had passed by for review. What was the out-
come? "But for Adam no suitable helper was found"
(Genesis 2:20).

One husband told me of his disappointing marriage.
He spoke highly of his wife's abilities and homemaking
skills. He said that she was a good mother. But when I
asked him, "Is she your best friend?" he replied, "No, and
that's the problem!" Your spouse should be the best and
most intimate friend you have on earth. Marriage is something less than God intended when it is not built on the
principle of intimate companionship.

How Sexual Experience Is to Be Conducted

A marriage is a commitment to have sex only with your
marital partner—no one else! Genesis 2:24 says the man
"shall be united to his wife." Marital fidelity is foundational
to a good marriage. How else can trust and dependence be
nurtured? There is no way to achieve sexual satisfaction
and the full giving of yourself to another person emotion-
ally and physically without fidelity. This is emphasized in
Proverbs 5:18-20:

May your fountain be blessed, and may you re-
joice in the wife of your youth. A loving doe, a
graceful deer—may her breasts satisfy you always, may you ever be captivated by her love.
Why be captivated, my son, by an adulteress?
Why embrace the bosom of another man's wife?

Marriage is the place for our sexual affections and desires to be fulfilled, nowhere else. Proverbs 6:32-35 reminds us of the heartaches in store for us if we fail to commit ourselves unreservedly to our marital partner:

But a man who commits adultery lacks judgment; whoever does so destroys himself. Blows
and disgrace are his lot, and his shame will never
be wiped away; for jealousy arouses a husband's
fury, and he will show no mercy when he takes
revenge. He will not accept any compensation;
he will refuse the bribe, however great it is.

Any marriage that tries to build itself on statements
such as "I will love you until I find someone else" has already planted seeds of destruction.

John and Susan seemed like an ideal couple, full of
happiness and fulfillment. So I was quite surprised when I
learned that Susan had been carrying on an affair for some
time. John knew nothing about it. She was tempted to tell
him and divorce him, but her vows kept her from that. She
realized that she had broken her vow to John by having sex
with another man, but filing for a divorce would be taking
things too far.

Her commitment, though weakened by prolonged un-
faithfulness, still reminded her that she was accountable
to God. It kept her from divorcing John. But interestingly, it
did not keep her from having sex with someone else. She
tried to justify herself by complaining that she had sexual
needs that her husband was not fulfilling.

When I reminded her that marriage is built on commitment to having sex with only your marital partner, she confessed her sin and agreed to break off the adulterous re-

lationship. She would try to restore her relationship with John. It came as a real shock to her husband, because he thought everything was fine between them. He found it hard to understand. But through much counseling he eventually realized his responsibility to fulfill his wife sexually. She seemed to be truly repentant and renewed her commitment to find fulfillment in her husband only.

The story is all too common these days. The secular world is constantly pressuring us to believe that God's standards are no longer relevant. They're outmoded, the world sneers—practically medieval.

But nothing has changed in God's mind. Marriage is still built on commitment—a commitment to have sex with your spouse only, and no one else!

A marriage is a sexual relationship without guilt, shame, or restriction. Genesis 2:25 says, "The man and his wife were both naked, and they felt no shame." Such freedom! They had no inhibitions, fears, or sexual misunderstandings. They were free to enjoy themselves and to explore their sexual desires.

A great deal of counseling today is aimed at correcting people's sexual fears. Sadly, many still view sex as something dirty or perverted—and indeed, it can be. But sex within marriage is never pictured that way. God puts his stamp of approval upon the sexual desires and acts of two people who are married to each other, who seek fulfillment within marriage.

One couple came to me for counseling after seven years of frustrating experiences in marriage. Both expressed their misunderstanding of sexual conduct within marriage. The wife kept saying, "He wants to do things that I don't think are right!" He replied, "Why are these things wrong?" As the discussion continued, it was obvious that they needed some biblical teaching about sex within marriage. Their problems included differing views about where and how sexual intercourse should take place and oral sex, among other things.

Hebrews 13:4 is an important verse in this area. It says:

> Marriage should be honored by all, and the mar-
> riage bed |Greek—*coitus*| kept pure, for God will
> judge the adulterer and all the sexually immoral.

Sexual experience outside of marriage is clearly wrong. But within marriage, God calls it "undefiled." You can't be guilty of something which is clearly acceptable to God. If you feel guilt for sexual activity within marriage, it must be "false guilt," a matter of your own feelings and under-standing—not that there is any sin involved.

Sin is lawlessness (1 John 3:4) or disobedience to the revealed law of God. Something is wrong when God says it's wrong. God makes it clear in the Bible what is right and what is wrong regarding sexual activity. Whatever we do that is not expressly forbidden in the Scriptures—by command or principle—is a matter of personal freedom and conscience.

We are free to do whatever is not forbidden by God, provided that we do not hurt others in the process. The Christian law of liberty and love is very careful to avoid causing another Christian brother or sister to fall or to violate his or her conscience (Romans 14:19-21; 1 Corin-thians 8:9-13). This certainly applies to husbands and wives.

What Are the Sexual Laws of God?

Our world suffers from a lack of authority. There is no moral direction. We do whatever pleases us, regardless of the consequences.

But God is a God of order and design. His laws were established to protect us, not to keep us from having fun. What he forbids is for our good. His restrictions provide for the greatest amount of happiness and fulfillment—and that includes the matter of sex.

Teachings of sexual freedom that encourage us to vio-late God's laws do not lead to freedom, but rather to bondage and a weakened sexual vibrancy and fulfillment. Profligacy diminishes sexual vitality. Yet from all we see and hear, you would think that sexual immorality would lead to ecstasies of sexual pleasure and fulfillment. There is a measure of sexual pleasure in acts that violate God's laws; but the consequences are devastating. The older you get, the more aware you are of how true that is!

We are warned against several sexual sins:

1. *Adultery* (Exodus 20:14; Leviticus 18:20; 20:10; Deuteronomy 22:22)
2. *Incest*—sex with blood relatives (Leviticus 18:6-18; 20:11-12, 14, 17, 19-21)
3. *Homosexuality* (Leviticus 18:22; 20:13)
4. *Bestiality*—sex with animals (Exodus 22:19; Leviticus 18:23; 20:15-16)
5. *Premarital sex* (Exodus 22:16-17; Deuteronomy 22:20-21, 23-29)
6. *Rape* (Deuteronomy 22:25-27)
7. *Prostitution* (Leviticus 19:29; 21:9; Deuteronomy 22:21; 23:17-18)

God gave us these laws to protect his original design for sex and marriage. We have inherited a desire to break God's laws. Although sexual desire was given to man and woman by God for our pleasure and for propagating the human race, sinful desire is something else. Perverted sexual desire is the intent to commit the sexual sins which God says are an abomination.

A Definition of Pornography

Pornography is the publication of materials that describe or picture sexual activity that God condemns. It is dangerous because it appeals to our sinful desires. The tendency to violate God's sexual laws is in each of our hearts, and pornography fans the flame of illicit passion. What we look at and concentrate on will begin to affect us, especially in times of temptation and provocation. It is much easier to fall into sexual sin when your mind has fantasized over pornographic material (whether magazines, movies, or books).

Our hedonistic culture tolerates pornographic material that once was considered wrong and which was banished from public view. Today it is accessible in our homes through cable television and video cassettes. Pornographic magazines can be found in respectable stores and newstands. There has been a massive breakdown of moral consciousness.

But God's sexual laws still stand. They have not changed.

The Seriousness of Sexual Sin

Human life was designed by God, made in his own image and after his likeness. The entrance of sin into the world has deeply affected his beautiful creation. Human existence has been infiltrated by a foreign power that continues to attack the fiber of what we are and what we should do. We think differently because of it, and we are often consumed with selfish interests rather than pleasing the God who made us, the God who knows us better than we know ourselves.

Violating God's sexual laws carries serious consequences. Continual disregard for them soon prompts us to ridicule divine laws and to assume that they were invented by religious groups who have deep inhibitions and fears about sex (and who, because of their beliefs, desire to impose these restrictions on others). Isn't religion always against having fun?

That's what a young college student tried to tell me. He had a deep hatred for the Bible and religion because of their attitudes toward sexual freedom. He believed that all of us should be free to do whatever we desire sexually, and that there are no consequences to face. How immature and foolish! There are consequences—and they are usually understood only after it is too late.

1. *Loss of sexual vitality.* Continual sexual sin leads to a loss of sexual vitality. Proverbs 5:9-10 speaks of this as it warns young men to avoid prostitutes:

> lest you give your best strength to others and your years to one who is cruel, lest strangers feast on your wealth and your toil enrich another man's house.

When a husband has sex with his wife, he is giving to himself, for they have become "one flesh" (Genesis 2:24). When a man has sex with someone other than his wife, he loses something; sexual energy and vitality are drained, never to be recovered again.

Our tragedy is that people neither understand this principle nor believe it to be true. There is a certain psychological and emotional release to sexual activity. But when it occurs outside of the marital bond, it tears down sexual ties rather than building them up. The result? The relationship deteriorates into animal passion and empty sexual gratification, demanding more and more while offering less and less. And that often leads to other sexual involvements and practices, all trying in vain to satisfy the longing of the soul.

Marital fidelity maintains sexual interest and vitality over many years, even though the physical body ages. The process of lovemaking may change in method or frequency, but sexual satisfaction is sustained because it is vitally related to faithfulness. There are serious consequences to sexual sin:

> Can a man scoop fire into his lap without his clothes being burned? Can a man walk on hot coals without his feet being scorched? So is he who sleeps with another man's wife; no one who touches her will go unpunished. (Proverbs 6:27-29).

While the Bible does not spell out what the punishment might be, it is clear there are terrible consequences.

2. *Loss of respect*. Many teenage girls have discovered too late that sexual sin results in a loss of respect. One girl told me how she was pressured by her boyfriend to have sex with him. He insisted that if she really loved him, she would do anything sexually to prove it. But that's not love; we could call it animal lust or selfish gratification, but it's not love. Love—God's kind of love—respects and honors God's laws and the person with whom you desire an intimate relationship. Love will not use a person merely to satisfy sexual desires. Love protects, defends, and builds on trust and fidelity. That's what Proverbs 6:32-33 means when it says:

> But a man who commits adultery lacks judgment; whoever does so destroys himself. Blows and disgrace are his lot, and his shame will never be wiped away.

Reputations, ministries, churches, and lives have been wrecked by sexual sin. The shame, disgrace, and heartache can continue for years. The loss is hard to recover, and were it not for the grace and forgiveness of God, the consequences would be even more serious.

This loss of respect is not just in the eyes of those you have offended or those who have learned of your sexual involvements. It also involves yourself. You lose respect for yourself because you failed to exercise the discipline needed to avoid sexual sin. Counseling has often uncovered serious problems of self-worth and self-image that have resulted from sexual sin. There is a price to be paid in how you view both yourself and the depth of your character.

3. *Sexual disease*. No subject generates as much angry rhetoric as the suggestion that sexual disease often invades the bodies of those who engage in continual sexual sin. If you have been guilty of sexual sin in the past, you know that you did not develop warts or any other immediate problem. This may have deceived you into thinking that there would never be any physical consequences.

The sad truth is that venereal disease has often been transmitted from an infected person to someone having sex for the first time. This is no laughing matter—it is a serious problem throughout the nation and the world.

Some biblical scholars and teachers believe that the following passages refer to just this:

> Proverbs 5:11—"At the end of your life you will groan, when your flesh and body are spent."
> Romans 1:27—"Men committed indecent acts with other men, and received in themselves the due penalty for their perversion."
> 1 Corinthians 6:18—"Flee from sexual immorality. All other sins a man commits are outside

his body, but he who sins sexually sins against
his own body."

Repeated sex with your marital partner does not cause
sexual disease, but such activity with someone other than
your spouse can. How do we explain this? Some try to
argue that various infections or menstrual difficulties in
married women reveal that the problem is simply a matter
of repeated sexual activity, occurring in married and unmar-
ried people alike.

But there is a vast difference—as any trained specialist
will tell you—between the normal difficulties of a married,
sexually faithful wife, and the typical sexual diseases that
afflict those engaged in sexual activities outside of marriage. Why argue about it? The facts are overwhelming! Sexual disease is much more likely to strike those who are involved in sexual sin!

4. *Loss of Christian fellowship and friendship.* An unbeliever
will find this point meaningless. But it is critically serious
for believers. Sexual sin damages and breaks our relationships with other Christians. Paul wrote about this to the
church of Corinth:

> But now I am writing you that you must not as-
> sociate with anyone who calls himself a brother
> but is sexually immoral or greedy, an idolater or
> a slanderer, a drunkard or a swindler. With such
> a man do not even eat. What business is it of
> mine to judge those outside the church? Are you
> not to judge those inside? God will judge those
> outside. "Expel the wicked man from among
> you" (1 Corinthians 5:11-13).

Many churches invite tragedy by ignoring their
spiritual responsibility to confront and discipline those living in sin. When Christians persist in sin, with no attitude
of repentance or desire for victory, they should be removed
from the fellowship of the church. Christians must avoid
being with them, even at mealtimes. That's strong language! But it demonstrates what God thinks of habitual sin
among his people.

51

5. *Eternal consequences*. The most serious consequence of sexual sin is that it often reveals that the guilty party is not a true believer. Such a person faces the eternal judgment of God.

"I warn you, as I did before, that those who live like this will not inherit the kingdom of God," Paul wrote in Galatians 5:21. What things? Verse 19 lists immorality, impurity, and debauchery, among other sins. Ephesians 5:5 adds,

> For of this you can be sure: No immoral, impure or greedy person—such a man is an idolater— has any inheritance in the kingdom of Christ and of God.

In speaking of the danger of sexual sin, Paul wrote to the Thessalonians that "in this matter no one should wrong his brother or take advantage of him. The Lord will punish men for all such sins, as we have already told you and warned you" (1 Thessalonians 4:6). Sodom and Gomorrah, Jude 7 says, "gave themselves up to sexual immorality and perversion. They serve as an example of those who suffer the punishment of eternal fire."

The last book of the Bible, Revelation, says that the "sexually immoral" shall have their final destiny "in the fiery lake of burning sulfur. This is the second death" (21:8). It goes on to say that those shut out of the heavenly city include "the sexually immoral" (22:15).

Is there any hope for those who commit sexual sin? Yes, thank God! The *only* hope for sinners of any stripe is faith in the substitutionary death of Jesus Christ over 1900 years ago. The Bible demands confession and repentance. A true believer's attitude toward sin and its consequences is different from that of the unbeliever.

One of the best biblical passages designed to give hope to those desiring to escape from the corruption of sin is found in 1 Corinthians 6:9-11:

> Do you not know that the wicked will not inherit the kingdom of God? Do not be deceived: Neither the sexually immoral nor idolaters nor adulterers nor male prostitutes nor homosexual

offenders nor thieves nor the greedy nor drunkards nor slanderers nor swindlers will inherit the kingdom of God. *And that is what some of you were.* But you were washed, you were sanctified, you were justified in the name of the Lord Jesus Christ and by the Spirit of our God.

What wonderful words of encouragement—"And that is what some of you *were*"! God is a God of forgiveness. He can cleanse you from your sin through the work of his Son, Jesus Christ, whose death on the cross was a sufficient payment for all your sin. If you have not done so, will you put your faith and trust in Jesus Christ? Will you now receive him into your heart as your Lord and Savior, trusting his work on the cross for you as your only hope of salvation? The songwriter of a well-known Christian song has put it this way:

> What can wash away my sin?
> Nothing but the blood of Jesus!
> What can make me whole again?
> Nothing but the blood of Jesus!
>
> Oh, precious is the flow
> That makes me white as snow;
> No other fount I know
> Nothing but the blood of Jesus!

4

WHAT HAPPENED TO THE FAMILY?

On March 27, 1983, an article appeared in the Santa Ana *Register* describing the revolution going on in family law. It reported that the nation's divorce rate doubled between 1966 and 1976, and claimed that 1982 saw more than one million divorces in the United States.

Professor Homer H. Clarke, Jr., of the University of Colorado law school, was quoted as saying, "All the old notions of how families ought to work and how people ought to behave have completely broken down. The only thing left to provide some kind of structure is law."

That same article reported that forty-eight out of our fifty states have eliminated any fault as grounds for divorce, and that the legal focus has shifted from moral to economic issues. What a commentary on our times!

If we can trust the accuracy of the 1980 census, more than one-half of all divorces involve couples with children. It is estimated that out of sixty-six million children under the age of eighteen, eleven to thirteen million are step-children. At present rates, one-half of the children in Los Angeles county alone will not be living with both of their natural parents by 1990. That's staggering!

A recent United Nations report said that the United States leads all nations on earth in the divorce rate. The United States Census Bureau tells us that the average marriage in America today lasts about seven years. The importance and structure of the family is under tremendous pressure today. Its very foundations are questioned and attacked.

Former president Jimmy Carter in 1980 established the White House Conference on the Family. It was meant to study carefully the problems of the family in this country and to recommend needed changes. Dr. James Dobson was quoted in the May 7, 1982, issue of *Christianity Today* concerning this event:

> The White House Conference was a disaster. The best thing about it was that most of its recommendations were not accepted or applied. Massive governmental programs were requested, costing untold billions of dollars and affecting every area of our lives. Most important, those programs would have brought the federal government into the family through the front door, which is what we least need at this time. I was able to coauthor a minority report in which I expressed this dissenting viewpoint during the final Task Force meetings.

Dr. Dobson is well known for his emphasis on the family. He insists that government has no answers. Our society is in desperate need of returning to the biblical foundations that established and supported the family from the beginning of time.

Who Invented the Family?

Who invented the family? Who created a family in the first place? Just try to explain that one if you leave out God! The Bible says it was God who created the first man and the first woman and it was God who gave the first instructions about having children.

> God blessed [Adam and Eve] and said to them, "Be fruitful and increase in number; fill the earth and subdue it. Rule over the fish of the sea and the birds of the air and over every living creature that moves on the ground" (Genesis 1:28).

Adam and Eve were obedient to this first command and became the parents of Cain (Genesis 4:1). Cain later acquired his brother when Abel was born (Genesis 4:2). Adam and Eve became parents for the third time in Genesis 4:25 when Eve gave birth to a son, Seth.

Without much fanfare or argument, the Bible speaks simply and beautifully of the beginning of family life. It uses words like *brother* and *son* and *father* and *wife*.

And a family is born.

How a Family Is Established

One simple verse of Scripture teaches three foundational principles about family life:

> For this reason a man will leave his father and mother and be united to his wife, and they will become one flesh (Genesis 2:24).

The three principles deal with (1) how a family is established, (2) how a marriage is determined, and (3) how sexual experience is to be conducted.

That simple verse explains several things:

1. A family is composed of a father and a mother.
2. To be a father or a mother necessitates a child.
3. A family unit is established the moment a couple is married.
4. In some sense, the man's relationship with his own parents (his original family) is severed the moment he gets married.

The most basic definition of a family includes three words: *father*, *mother*, and *child*. When the child gets married, it is necessary to "leave" and "cleave," and a new family unit becomes possible. The parents must continue to be respected and honored, but the child's relationship to them is severed the moment he or she is married. Surely the child remains the child of those parents forever. But the responsibility to remain under their authority and direct influence ends when the child marries.

WHERE DO I COME FROM?

In a strict sense, there is no family if there is no father or mother. Two men do not make a family. A husband is not a father until he has a son or daughter (likewise for the wife and mother). Divorce or death can eliminate one of the parents, but the family—composed of a father and a mother—at some point existed.

A mother and a son are still a family even though the father dies; the family began when there was a father and a mother. A single person may become an "instant parent" through adoption, but the fact remains that the true parents are the original father and mother. We may use the word *family* to describe a multitude of human relationships, but the original institution designed by God was composed of father, mother, and child.

In conversing with a young man in his twenties, I discovered that he fathered a child a couple of years prior to our meeting, but left his wife and child in another state some two thousand miles away. When I asked him about it, he became defensive and tried to explain that it was a "mistake" and that it was not really his family.

"Did you get married to that girl?" I asked. "Yes, but . . ." he replied. Before he could finish, I said, "And did you have a child by your wife?" "Yes, but . . ." I stopped him again, and said, "Then you have a family no matter what you are trying to say!" It soon became clear that he was simply trying to convince himself that it was not true, even though he knew in his heart that it was. He was both a husband and a father, and despite his insecurity and his desire to get out of his responsibilities and start over again, I continued to emphasize that the wife and child in another state were still his family.

Fortunately, the story ended on a good note as this young man returned to his wife and child, got a job, began supporting his family, and has been grateful ever since for our conversation that day.

The story could be repeated over and over again. Many fathers ignore their family responsibilities. They try to run away and "start all over again." They move to another city or state and try to forget the people they left behind. I often hear stories that indicate a shift in thinking has taken place in our culture. The sense of family has so deteriorated that people abandon their home responsibilities and accountability.

I've also noticed changing attitudes toward children. Many parents see them as burdens instead of blessings. They think of them as mistakes and wish that they had never had a child in the first place. Our obsession with individual freedom has removed words like *altruism* and *duty* from our vocabulary.

But God's standards have not changed. A family consists of a father, mother, and child. Care of the family is a serious duty, not to be treated lightly. Consider 1 Timothy 5:8:

> If anyone does not provide for his relatives, and especially for his immediate family, he has denied the faith and is worse than an unbeliever.

Even unbelievers can demonstrate loyalty to the family. The Bible has no sympathy for a parent who abandons family responsibility. That's why marriage and parenting involve crucial decisions which require a clear understanding of and commitment to the responsibilities they demand.

A New Beginning

A list of families follows the accounts of Adam and Eve, and we assume that the earth's population grew tremendously. But so did the wickedness of man.

> The LORD saw how great man's wickedness on the earth had become, and that every inclination of the thoughts of his heart was only evil all the time (Genesis 6:5).

The sins of mankind prompted God to destroy the human race with a flood. It became necessary to start all over again. God started again with a family: Noah, his wife, his three sons, and their wives. Genesis 7:1 says:

> The LORD then said to Noah, "Go into the ark, you and your whole family, because I have found you righteous in this generation."

WHERE DO I COME FROM?

God repeated to Noah and his family the original command given to Adam and Eve about propagating the human race (Genesis 9:1). Noah and his family were to "be fruitful and increase in number and fill the earth."

Genesis 10 gives a genealogical list of how Noah and his sons took God's commands seriously. And there is an interesting statement following each mention of the descendants of Noah's three sons. In verses 5, 20, and 31 (NASB), we read that these descendants were separated into lands, languages, nations, and *families*. A final summary of these descendants is found in Genesis 10:32 (NASB), which begins, "These are the *families* of the sons of Noah." The population of our planet after the flood was divided into families. We cannot doubt it—the family was an institution designed by God and foundational to the fabric of human society.

This might seem elementary. Some may think, "How simple can you get? Isn't it obvious to everyone that the basic unit of society is the family?"

Evidently not. Many countries today are trying to eliminate the family as the basic unit of society, replacing it with the state or government. Talk about the "family of man" too often aims at demeaning or eliminating the traditional family composed of father, mother, and child.

This characterizes much of the teaching of communism and certain religious cults that demand allegiance to a leader, often at the sacrifice of your own family. Even in a democratic society like the United States, the government does not always protect the family. Sometimes it undermines the home by its decisions. The government or society tries to become the family. But according to the Bible, the family is a father, mother, and child. Nothing has changed that.

The Role of the Father

A young father asked me, "What is a father supposed to do?" I spent a few minutes with him that day explaining from the Bible what his duties were. He was amazed. His wife had been "on his case" (according to him) about being a father. He was never trained about what to do, and he did not know where to start.

The story is common. We grow up expecting that we will understand what to do when the time comes. But many mistakes and ruined lives are bound to multiply where there is no clear understanding of the role fathers are to fulfill.

The Old Testament uses the word *father* nearly 1,200 times, while the New Testament equivalent appears 418 times. Ancient cultures always considered the father to be the head of his family or his house. Joshua was a good example of that when he spoke to the children of Israel:

> And if it is disagreeable in your sight to serve the LORD, choose for yourselves today whom you will serve: whether the gods which your *fathers* served which were beyond the River, or the gods of the Amorites, in whose land you are living; but as for *me and my house, we will serve the* LORD (Joshua 24:15 NASB).

Joshua declared that he was the leader and head of his family regarding their spiritual loyalties and commitments.

The father was clearly the spiritual leader and the one from whom the sons would receive direction and blessing. In Genesis 27 we have the story of Isaac blessing his two sons, Jacob and Esau. In Genesis 48, Jacob blesses his son, Joseph, and his grandsons, Ephraim and Manasseh. In fact, we are told that Jacob blessed each of his sons:

> All these are the twelve tribes of Israel, and this is what their father said to them when he blessed them, giving each the blessing appropriate to him (Genesis 49:28).

The father is clearly the spiritual leader of the family. And with that role comes an awesome responsibility—to teach your children.

Deuteronomy 6 is a tremendous chapter to help fathers understand their responsibility to their children:

> These are the commands, decrees and laws the LORD your God directed me to teach you to

observe in the land that you are crossing the Jordan to possess, so that you, your children and their children after them may fear the LORD your God as long as you live by keeping all his decrees and commands that I give you, and so that you may enjoy long life (vv. 1, 2).

Fathers are clearly responsible to teach their children the ways and commands of the Lord. It is not to be left to the church or to the school—it is the duty of fathers! And to be adequately prepared for the task, several things are essential:

1. *An intense love for God Himself.* Deuteronomy 6:5 says, "Love the LORD your God will *all* your heart and with *all* your soul and with *all* your strength." Jesus called this the greatest commandment of all (Matthew 22:37-38). Fathers cannot be the spiritual leaders and teachers of their children without it. When a father neglects his relationship to God, the family suffers. It's as simple—and as dreadful—as that. There's no real authority in the home once the father abandons his love for God Himself. It is the rock upon which a family is built.

John was a conscientious father, but his children were not responding. His wife, Mary, continued to worry about his relationship with the Lord. He said that it didn't matter what he did . . . but things got increasingly worse in their home. One day he came to talk. He was ready. Concerned about losing his children's respect and response, he asked, "What's wrong?" He seemed surprised when I asked him about his commitment to God. Why would I connect that with the problems he was having?

But when I pointed out this verse from Deuteronomy 6:5, he immediately confessed, "That's not where I am." After further conversation, he realized that if he was to be the spiritual leader and teacher of his children, he desperately needed to love God with all his heart, soul, and mind. He loved his kids, surely—but without his total commitment to God, the children had no example to follow.

2. *An inward commitment to the commands of God.* How many times we hear it said, "Don't do what I do—do what I say!"

WHAT HAPPENED TO THE FAMILY?

Our children, however, see what we do, and that speaks louder than all we say. Deuteronomy 6:6 says, "These commandments that I give you today are to be *upon your hearts*." There's where the problem often lies—"on the heart" of the father. Fathers cannot teach effectively if they are not personally committed to what they tell their children. No issue of the family is any greater or more serious than this one.

I was talking to a young teenaged girl about her smoking habit. Her father said, "I don't understand why she is doing that! We do not want her to do it, and we have often warned her about it and the damage it will bring to her health." I said, "Sir, do you smoke?" He replied, "What has that got to do with it?" The fact is, it has everything to do with it! The father's smoking habit was a greater message to his daughter than all his warnings to her about the dangers of smoking.

It is true that there is no specific command of God about smoking. This is not surprising, since the filthy practice was invented in relatively modern times. But we are exhorted to take care of our bodies. And how shall our children listen to that exhortation if we do not practice it ourselves? When fathers have no inward commitment to what God says and commands, they cannot expect their children to obey God's commands, either.

3. A *constant communication with your children about what God says and commands*. Consider these words from Deuteronomy 6:7-9:

> Impress them on your children. Talk about them when you sit at home and when you walk along the road, when you lie down and when you get up. Tie them as symbols on your hands and bind them on your foreheads. Write them on the doorframes of your houses and on your gates.

Fathers must continually speak to their children of God's commands and principles. They should talk about them in every room of the house and at all times of the day. They must continually be teachers of their children; and though that role may be *supported* by others, it must never be *supplanted*!

A famous verse says, "Train a child in the way he should go, and when he is old he will not turn from it" (Proverbs 22:6). The word *train* primarily means "to dedicate." It is used in the Bible of dedicating things to God: a new house, the altar in the temple, the temple of Solomon, the house of God after the return of the Jews from the Babylonian captivity, and the wall of Jerusalem in the days of Nehemiah. It is used of training servants for battle (Genesis 14:14).

"To dedicate" implies the initiation of something. The father initiates in the life of his child the "way" in which the child should go. It is not the way the father wants him to go, but the way in which God wants him to go. "When the child is old" implies that the child is no longer a dependent and is now away from the father's influence. That child will not depart from the teaching of the father when he grows old. It will stay with him all his days.

These verses (and many more like them) emphasize that a father's primary responsibility—in addition to being the head of the family—is to teach and train his children.

What about Discipline?

Many discussions about the family and the role of the father center on discipline, whether the lack of it or the abuse of it. Discipline is critical to all of us. It is designed to prevent us from having wrong attitudes toward authority, and to provide us with the experiences that develop maturity. Undisciplined people are rebellious and immature.

The question often comes up: Are fathers instructed by God to spank? The following verses should help clarify the matter:

> Proverbs 13:24—"He who spares the rod hates his son, but he who loves him is careful to discipline him."
>
> Proverbs 22:15—"Folly is bound up in the heart of a child, but the rod of discipline will drive it far from him."
>
> Proverbs 23:13-14—"Do not withhold discipline from a child; if you punish him with the rod, he will not die. Punish him with the rod and save his soul from death."

> Proverbs 29:15—"The rod of correction imparts wisdom, but a child left to itself disgraces his mother."
>
> Proverbs 29:17—"Discipline your son, and he will give you peace; he will bring delight to your soul."

Now, let's be honest: Don't some of these statements appear to recommend child abuse? Are we to "beat" our children? Are we to use a "rod"? We need to get one thing straight right away—the Bible *never* condones child abuse. Discipline is one thing, but abuse is another. Parental discipline in terms of corporal punishment (spanking) should be applied to the buttocks of the child, and no place else!

The Bible warns fathers to avoid anger when they discipline their children (Ephesians 6:4). Angry fathers can lose control and become abusive—and that is sin. Colossians 3:21 indicates that youngsters can become discouraged by improper discipline. Discipline should be prayerfully and carefully applied, without anger. As a child gets older, the discipline must change from physical punishment (spanking) to restrictive punishment (limited phone calls, dates, use of car, and so on).

I shudder when parents tell me that they love their children too much to spank them. Time has revealed that undisciplined children become heartaches to their parents.

Twenty years ago, I had just that experience. Some parents I knew said they did not believe in spanking or in the concept of discipline. I warned them from the Bible about the dangers of such beliefs, and of the possible results to expect. They would not believe it.

They have lived to regret their decision. All three of their children are rebellious and scoff at their parents' authority and beliefs. It's a sad story, repeated too often. The Bible teaches that discipline reveals love, and that refusing to exercise it proves a lack of love.

The Role of the Mother

I find it interesting that the Bible does not give us many insights or commands for the mother. It almost appears that the major responsibility of raising children falls on the father rather than the mother. Perhaps the reason for this is that mothers have a natural tendency to love, care, protect, teach, warn, and worry! Fathers may often show disinterest and lack of responsibility toward their children. It shouldn't be that way, but it often is.

So what specific tasks does the Bible assign to mothers? Titus 2:4-5 lists some of them:

> Then they can train the younger women to love their husbands and children, to be self-controlled and pure, to be busy at home, to be kind, and to be subject to their husbands, so that no one will malign the word of God.

Mothers are to love their children. The Greek word for *love* used here implies friendship or companionship. It is the love that is always there, alongside of, helping, encouraging, and supporting. The phrase "to be busy at home" emphasizes the importance of the home to the well-being and security of the family, and that mothers must pay special attention to the place we call "home." It does not forbid mothers from working, but it does say that the home should be a priority.

Some of our current thinking is undermining God's original intention for the family. A family is composed of a father (who serves as head of the household, the spiritual guide and teacher of his family), a mother (who loves her children, constantly encouraging and supporting them, making her home a priority), and a child (who receives the benefits of such parents).

The Role of Children

But what about the child? Does he or she have any special role to play in making the family what God intended it to be? The answer is an emphatic yes! God gives children specific responsibilities in the family. Some of these include:

1. *Respect for the parents.* "Honor your father and your mother, so that you may live long in the land the LORD your God is giving you," says Exodus 20:12. The principle is re-

peated in the New Testament. When children honor their parents, they will always speak well of them to others. If they do not, serious consequences can be expected. "If a man curses his father or mother, his lamp will be snuffed out in pitch darkness," says Proverbs 20:20. God calls a son "foolish" if he despises or looks down on his mother (Proverbs 15:20). Proverbs 19:26 adds, "He who robs his father and drives out his mother is a son who brings shame and disgrace."

2. *Obedience to the parents' authority*. Obedience involves listening as well as carrying out what was instructed. Proverbs 13:1 tells us that "A wise son heeds his father's instruction, but a mocker does not listen to rebuke." A child may not agree with a parent, but the child must listen and obey. Obedience is commanded in both testaments. Ephesians 6:1 says that children are to obey simply because it is the right thing to do. Colossians 3:20 says that it is necessary for children to obey if they want to please God.

The whole idea of a family from God's point of view is destroyed when children disobey their parents. Under the laws of the Old Testament, rebellion against parents was punished by stoning to death (Deuteronomy 21:18-21)! That's an incredible fact in light of secular thinking today.

In our day, children are often encouraged to spurn their parents. It is the "in thing" to do. A child who obeys his parents and who submits to their authority may be looked on with suspicion, sometimes mocked and made the butt of jokes. Many children laugh at and ridicule their parents because they see it portrayed that way on television and in movies. They begin to think that everyone's parents are stupid and unrelated to life. They can't cope with pressure and they certainly cannot understand kids!

It's different in the Bible. Elderly people are honored, not laughed at. Consider these passages:

> Proverbs 16:31—"Gray hair is a crown of splendor; it is attained by a righteous life."
>
> Proverbs 17:6—"Children's children are a crown to the aged, and parents are the pride of their children."

WHERE DO I COME FROM?

Proverbs 20:29—"The glory of young men is their strength, gray hair the splendor of the old."

Proverbs 23:22—"Listen to your father, who gave you life, and do not despise your mother when she is old."

Our culture suffers from many problems with family life. With so many families breaking up, shouldn't we start asking some serious questions about our attitudes and beliefs about the family? Do we agree with the Bible?

God's design for the human race involves the family in a deep and rich way. People and cultures lose their sense of direction and meaning when the family is destroyed or changed from what God intended. The family is the basic unit of society—it is the most important institution of man, rooted in and built upon the institution of marriage.

PART TWO

WHAT DIFFERENCE DOES IT MAKE?

Is the only goal in life "doing your own thing" or "getting to know yourself"? Are we the master of our own fate, the controllers of our destiny? Where does God fit in?

No doubt about it—selfism is a doctrine implicit in modern culture. It's the consumer philosophy par excellence. It attracts those with money and leisure. I find that to please myself comes naturally. It's not hard to accept the ideas of those who tell me how great I am and how I deserve much more than I have so far obtained in life.

But inside, such thinking doesn't produce the desired result. Instead of being satisfied, the thirst for more produces restlessness and emotional turmoil. Acquiring the "goodies" does not bring peace of mind and meaning to my life. Something more is needed.

David L. Hocking, *Pleasing God*

CHAPTER

5

AM I GOOD, BAD, OR BOTH?

Our lives have been deeply affected by what happened in the beginning moments of human history. Though men and women were created in the image of God, the vile effects of the sin they committed began to alter their value system. God's marvelous evaluation of the original creation ("it was very good") was marred by the effects which rebellion had upon his work.

The great question remains: To what extent has humanity been spoiled by sin? Philosophers and theologians throughout the centuries have wrestled with that problem. Is man innately good and thus capable of many wonderful deeds and thoughts? Or is he inherently evil, corrupted in all his thoughts and achievements? Some insist that he is both.

Although we are quite sure that something is deeply wrong with our culture, our society seems to have no desire to deal with it. The great American dream often has been wrecked by perversion and immorality. Dr. Karl Menninger concludes his excellent book, *Whatever Became of Sin?*, by writing:

> Neither theologian nor prophet nor sociologist, I am a doctor, speaking the medical tongue with a psychiatric accent. For doctors, health is the ultimate good, the ideal state of being. And mental health—some of us believe—includes all the healths: physical, social, cultural, and moral

(spiritual). To live, to love, to care, to enjoy, to build on the foundations of our predecessors, to revere the constant miracles of creation and endurance, of "the starry skies above and the moral law within"—these are acts and attitudes which express our mental health. Yet how is it, as Socrates wondered, that "men know what is good, but do what is bad"?[1]

Values are rooted in this question about the depravity of human life. We cannot begin to think of self-worth and human dignity until we first of all understand man's nature—is it good, bad, or both?

Earlier we talked about the presence of sin in our world. We investigated its cause and how man and woman were tempted by it in the first place. We argued from the Bible that humankind has indeed fallen into sin. Our experience tells us the same thing. It will do us no good to deny that something awful and tragic has happened to the human heart. The question is, how serious is it?

The Immediate Consequences for Adam and Eve

The first consequence of Adam and Eve's sin seems to be shame. Genesis 3:7 (NASB) says, "Then the eyes of both of them were opened, and they knew that they were naked." The Hebrew word translated *knew* refers not only to knowledge of facts, but to profound inward experience. The intimacy of a husband's sexual relationship with his wife is described in the Bible with this same Hebrew word.

In the depths of their souls, Adam and Eve had an acute consciousness of shame and sin. They knew that something was wrong. What was their immediate reaction? "They sewed fig leaves together and made coverings for themselves." They tried to hide their shame with shabby little pieces of vegetation!

Sin today brings the same sense of ruin. There are few who feel no immediate shame when their wrongdoings are discovered and exposed. But that inward shame and embarrassment quickly turns to self-defense in an attempt to cover what was done. We frantically try to justify our sin to ourselves as well as to others.

It is important for us to understand that Adam and Eve did not merely *think* that something was wrong—they knew it in their hearts! Their attempt to cover what they felt was simply the normal way that we, too, handle the guilt that lodges in the depths of our souls.

That first couple did not merely try to hide their shame. They also looked for ways to excuse it. The condition of our own hearts is very often revealed in this same way. Rather than be honest about what we have done, our shame and embarrassment prompt us to deceive and lie. The easiest way to relieve the pain we feel inside is to place the blame on anything or anyone other than ourselves.

Genesis 3:12-13 tells us how Adam and Eve handled their sin when confronted with it by the Lord God:

> The man said, "The woman you put here with me—she gave me some fruit from the tree, and I ate it." Then the LORD God said to the woman, "What is this you have done?" The woman said, "The serpent deceived me, and I ate."

Adam blamed his wife. Eve blamed the devil. Today we have T-shirts that proclaim, "The devil made me do it!"

All of this shame, hiding, and blaming did nothing to change the facts. Adam and Eve had sinned, and their environment, beliefs, values, and abilities were forever changed. Nothing would ever be the same again. The beauty and joy of their garden paradise vanished. They forfeited both fellowship and enjoyment. They were expelled from Eden because of their sin: "So the LORD God banished him from the Garden of Eden" (Genesis 3:23). When the couple tried to stay, God had no other choice but to forcibly drive them out (Genesis 3:24).

Adam and Eve's sin so radically polluted everything around them that even the ground itself was cursed:

> Cursed is the ground because of you; through painful toil you will eat of it all the days of your life. It will produce thorns and thistles for you, and you will eat the plants of the field. By the

sweat of your brow you will eat your food
(Genesis 3:17-19).

There is a certain therapy in being outdoors, working in the dirt, trimming the bushes, planting shrubs and flowers. But I hate weeds, and I'm not thrilled about gardening because of them. Why do those weeds have to spoil it all? No sooner have I gotten my garden cleaned out, than the weeds start marching back!

I love the beauty and the smell of a rose, but the thorns are there also—a reminder that Adam and Eve's sin still carries consequences.

One commentator said this about the curse:

The material object of the temptation was taken from the vegetable kingdom, the instrument of the tempter from the animal kingdom. Therefore, both vegetable and animal remain under the curse; and the creation, which through man should have advanced to redemption and perfection, remains until now subject to vanity.[2]

It's important for us to understand what happened to Adam and Eve *immediately* when they sinned. I can think of at least three things:

1. A feeling of shame that prompted an attempt to hide and cover their sin.
2. An attempt to blame someone else for what they had done.
3. A loss of fellowship with God and enjoyment of their environment.

These consequences aren't restricted to Adam and Eve. John Henderson experienced all three.

John stole large sums of money from his company. According to his own testimony, he felt shame the first time he did it. But the more he did it, the less shame he felt. Then one day he was exposed. In that moment he felt great shame and immediately tried to cover up what he had done. His cover-up led him through many lies, all of which he tried to justify. It was self-protection!

When the evidence finally stacked up against him, he began blaming others and pointing to situations within the company. He no longer enjoyed his job, and his relationships with fellow employees nose dived. Then he was fired and disgraced.

It's tough to pick up the pieces of such an experience and put one's life back together again. John was able to do it; but many never see that moment come. Their lives are permanently scarred.

What Do We Mean by Depravity?

What do we mean when we talk about "depravity"? Some speak of "total depravity." They believe that mankind is, at bottom, evil and not good. It isn't that we cannot do good, but that we cannot do anything that is truly good in the sight of God which would please him and give him glory. The most wicked among us have some human good in them.

When we measure ourselves by ourselves, we can always find some good in us. But that is not how God judges us. His standards are different. Humankind, according to the Bible, is incapable of doing anything or desiring anything that is pleasing to God. The best among us has impure motives for the good we do. We seem programmed to do human good only for our own glory—or worse yet, for Satan—but never for the glory of our Creator.

Total depravity means that everything about us— mind, emotions, will—has been corrupted by sin. The Bible speaks of sin in our lives as being centered in the "heart." It is not that our bodies themselves are evil. Our eyes, hands, feet, are sometimes described in the Bible as "instruments" of evil, but they are not evil in themselves (see Romans 6:13, 19).

Sin in the Heart

When we talk about someone's heart, we refer to his or her personality. It is in the heart that the Bible says sin lives. In a classic and wonderful book by the seventeenth-century theologian John Owen, we found these remarks about sin in the heart:

75

In Scripture the heart is variously used as a synonym—sometimes for the mind and understanding, sometimes for the will, sometimes for the conscience, and sometimes for the whole soul. Generally, it denotes the whole soul of man and all the faculties of it. But the faculties change with the focus, so it is the mind which inquires what is good or evil and judges ethically what shall be done or refused. The affections like or dislike, cleaving to one or having aversion to another. The conscience warns and determines. All are aspects of the heart, and it is in this sense that we say the seat and subject of this law of sin is the heart of man.[3]

Depravity means that there is sin in our hearts. It causes deceitfulness, making great contradictions occur in someone's life. We have no knowledge of how it works, how insidious it is, or how damaging it can be. We are constantly tricked by its impulses and the many promises which it makes. The heart is uncertain in what it does and false in what it promises.

Inability to Do Good in the Sight of God

We cannot do good in the sight of God. Romans 3:10-12 quotes Psalm 14 and 53 when it says:

There is no one righteous, not even one; there is no one who understands, no one who seeks God. All have turned away, they have together become worthless; there is no one who does good, not even one.

There can be no doubt that this is God's own viewpoint. Both Psalms 14 and 53 say that "God looks down from heaven on the sons of men to see if there are any who understand, any who seek God." What he saw is that there is no one like that. And just to make sure we don't miss the point, Isaiah writes:

All of us have become like one who is unclean, and all our righteous acts are like filthy rags; we all shrivel up like a leaf, and like the wind our sins sweep us away (Isaiah 64:6).

From God's point of view, none of us are righteous, and all of our human good is like a filthy garment. Romans 3:23 concludes, "for all have sinned and fall short of the glory of God."

Inability to Understand Spiritual Truth

There is another consequence to our depraved condition: We cannot understand spiritual truth. We have a blind spot when it comes to the things of God. "The man without the Spirit does not accept the things that come from the Spirit of God, for they are foolishness to him, and he cannot understand them, because they are spiritually discerned" (1 Corinthians 2:14).

It's not simply that we don't want to understand spiritual things. The Bible says that we cannot understand them. Depravity affects our ability to grasp spiritual truth. Jesus said in John 8:43, "Why is my language not clear to you? Because you are unable to hear what I say."

Spiritually Dead

Death is a consequence of sin. We all will die physically because of both Adam's sin and our own. But there is something else about depravity that often escapes our notice. The Bible describes people without Christ as spiritually dead.

> As for you, you were dead in your transgressions and sins, in which you used to live when you followed the ways of this world and of the ruler of the kingdom of the air, the spirit who is now at work in those who are disobedient. All of us also lived among them at one time, gratifying the cravings of our sinful nature and following its desires and thoughts (Ephesians 2:1-3).

We shudder at the description of what we once were: "dead in transgressions and sins," "those who are disobedient," "by nature objects of wrath." That's depravity! Because we are spiritually dead, we are unable to save ourselves or respond to God as he desires. Isaiah wrote about that:

> But your iniquities have separated you from you God; your sins have hidden his face from you, so that he will not hear (Isaiah 59:2).

Romans 5:12 tells us that through Adam's sin death has come to everyone. Romans 6:23 tells us that the wages of sin is death. Because we are spiritually dead we cannot respond rightly to the God who made us. That is the tragedy of depravity.

Depravity means that every person has sinned and is capable of the worst sins. It means that our whole personality has been affected by sin and that in our hearts we are constantly being deceived and manipulated by sin. Unbelievers cannot do good for the glory of God.

Depravity means that we cannot understand spiritual truth or respond to God without God's help and intervention. We cannot save ourselves or improve ourselves to God's standards of righteousness. We are spiritually separated from God, and our sin blinds us to it.

Without God, our values are warped and fall incredibly short of God's will and purposes. We become arrogant, proud of our own abilities and achievements, which leads to self-righteousness. We redefine sin. We become tolerant of the sins which God condemns. We compromise with what God hates, and we learn to defend and justify our actions.

Depravity Is Like the Law

The apostle Paul made a brilliant analysis of our depraved condition when he wrote:

> For what I want to do I do not do, but what I hate I do. And if I do what I do not want to do, I agree that the law is good. As it is, it is no longer I myself who do it, but it is sin living in me. I know that nothing good lives in me, that is, in my sinful nature. For I have the desire to do what is good, but I cannot carry it out. For what I do is not the good I want to do; no, the evil I do not

want to do—this I keep on doing. Now if I do what I do not want to do, it is no longer I who do it, but it is sin living in me that does it.

So I find this law at work: When I want to do good, evil is right there with me. For in my inner being I delight in God's law; but I see another law at work in the members of my body, waging war against the law of my mind and making me a prisoner of the law of sin at work within my members. What a wretched man I am! Who will rescue me from this body of death? Thanks be to God—through Jesus Christ our Lord!

So then, I myself in my mind am a slave to God's law, but in the sinful nature a slave to the law of sin (Romans 7:15-25).

Sin dominates and controls our lives. As a law, it demands obedience. It also rewards and punishes like the law. This law of sin dwells in our hearts. It never leaves us this side of heaven. Paul says that when you want to do something good, evil is present. It controls our motives, desires, and thoughts. It confuses our good intentions and drags us down when we desire to soar to spiritual heights. It uses our good desires to its evil ends. It constantly thwarts our moves toward God, and tempts us to satisfy ourselves at the expense of others. No wonder that Paul cried out, "What a wretched man I am!"

What Benefits Come from Understanding Our Depravity?

Mulling over depravity can leave you depressed for weeks. Is there no hope? Of course there is! God's grace, love, mercy, and forgiveness have made it possible for us to recover. Deliverance is possible through the death and resurrection of Jesus Christ. He died for our sins. He paid the penalty and consequence for our depravity. He can set us free! The good news is the gospel of Jesus Christ our Lord—not the latest book on how wonderful we are.

We can, however, profit from considering our natural state. We can gain:

1. A profound sense of humility.
2. A deep realization of our need for a savior.
3. A clear recognition of guilt.
4. A dependency upon God.
5. A loving and understanding heart toward others.
6. A willingness to forgive.

A Profound Sense of Humility

When we know our own hearts in the way the Bible knows us, there is no room for self-righteousness or moral arrogance. When a friend commits adultery, humility says, "Except for the grace of God, that could have been me."

Jesus once taught a parable about two men who went into the temple to pray. The parable was directed to those "who were confident of their own righteousness and looked down on everybody else" (Luke 18:9). Jesus contrasted a Pharisee with a tax-gatherer—who was hated by the people, usually filled with avarice and greed, and who often cheated the people by charging too much tax and pocketing the difference.

> "The Pharisee stood up and prayed about himself: 'God, I thank you that I am not like all other men—robbers, evildoers, adulterers—or even like this tax collector. I fast twice a week and give a tenth of all I get.'
>
> "But the tax collector stood at a distance. He would not even look up to heaven, but beat his breast and said, 'God, have mercy on me, a sinner.'
>
> "I tell you that this man, rather than the other, went home justified before God. For everyone who exalts himself will be humbled, and he who humbles himself will be exalted" (Luke 18:11-14).

A profound sense of humility had gripped the heart of this tax-gatherer. He knew that he was a sinner and confessed it before God. His sense of shame and guilt kept him from lifting his eyes to heaven. Instead he beat his breast in agony of soul, deeply feeling the conviction of God for all that he had done. And that humility was greatly honored by Christ.

A Deep Realization of Our Need for a Savior

When Paul cried out in Romans 7:24, "What a wretched man I am! Who will rescue me from this body of death?" his response was an emotional outburst of praise to the only Savior with power over sin: "Thanks be to God—through Jesus Christ our Lord!" (Romans 7:25).

John the Baptist, a great prophet and powerful preacher of repentance, knew that Jesus Christ was the only answer to the sin of the world. He said in John 1:29, "Look, the Lamb of God, who takes away the sin of the world!"

Isaiah 53:4-6 gives a prophecy about our Savior:

> Surely he took up our infirmities and carried our sorrows, yet we considered him stricken by God, smitten by him, and afflicted. But he was pierced for our transgressions, he was crushed for our iniquities; the punishment that brought us peace was upon him, and by his wounds we are healed. We all, like sheep, have gone astray, each of us has turned to his own way; and the LORD has laid on him the iniquity of us all.

1 Peter 2:24 adds, "He himself bore our sins in his body on the tree, so that we might die to sins and live for righteousness; by his wounds you have been healed."

One of the roughest, vilest, and most despicable jobs in the ancient world was to be a jailer. The men who oversaw these places were themselves worthy of being locked up. A story is told in Acts 16 of such a man who sensed his great need for a savior. An earthquake had broken the shackles of all his prisoners, and the jailhouse doors were flung open. The jailer, fearing the punishment his superiors would give him, was about to take his own life when Paul and Silas (who were prisoners) stopped him. He fell down before them and said, "Sirs, what must I do to be saved?"

That important question—which all of us need to ask at some point in our lives—was answered like this:

WHAT DIFFERENCE DOES IT MAKE?

> Believe in the Lord Jesus, and you will be saved—you and your household (Acts 16:31).

It is those who are most aware of their wretched heart who most deeply realize their need for a savior. Jesus made the point clear when he forgave the sins of a prostitute in Luke 7:47. And what did he say to the self-righteous Pharisee who was upset over his loving treatment of this woman?

> Therefore, I tell you, her many sins have been forgiven—for she loved much. But he who has been forgiven little loves little.

A Clear Recognition of Guilt

Clearly understanding depravity helps us to recognize what guilt is—not the false guilt of "feeling guilty" for something you have never done, but the true guilt based on what God says about our depravity.

The Bible says that guilt comes from violating the law of God. Sin is a transgression of God's law (1 John 3:4). The sin in our hearts makes us guilty before God. If I have violated one of God's laws, then I am guilty. Something is wrong because God says it is wrong, not because you or I or anyone else thinks it's wrong.

When a person recognizes his or her guilt before God, there can be no blaming the circumstances, environment, or other people. We simply respond, "I am guilty."

Now, it is possible to suffer from false guilt, a feeling arising from a misunderstanding of depravity. You feel guilty, but you really are not guilty at all.

Bruce Narramore and Bill Counts write about this problem in their book *Guilt and Freedom*:

> But not once does the Bible encourage believers in Jesus Christ to accept psychological guilt. Not once are Christians commanded to have a fear of punishment, a sense of worthlessness, or a feeling of rejection.[4]

The depravity of our heart causes us to sin in thought, word, and deed. Sin brings guilt. It is foolish to run away, and denial does not resolve it—only a savior can! And his forgiveness is complete, his cleansing total!

A Dependency upon God

Because I know what I'm really like, and because I understand the enormity of my heart's deceitfulness and depravity, I am forced to depend upon the grace, forgiveness, mercy, and power of God. I cannot make it without him. And do you know what? His heart delights that you feel that tremendous need of his help.

The very fact that we *are* sinful and so often tempted to sin is the reason God has invited us to come to him for help. When we are feeling particularly discouraged, it is not a bad idea to run to these beautiful words given in the book of Hebrews:

> For we do not have a high priest who is unable to sympathize with our weaknesses, but we have one who has been tempted in every way, just as we are—yet was without sin. Let us then approach the throne of grace with confidence, so that we may receive mercy and find grace to help us in our time of need (Hebrews 4:15,16).

King David understood his need to depend upon the Lord:

> O LORD, hear my prayer, listen to my cry for mercy; in your faithfulness and righteousness come to my relief. Do not bring your servant into judgment, for no one living is righteous before you (Psalm 143:1-2).

"No one living is righteous," David cried. Therefore, what should we do? What *can* we do? Call upon the Lord!

David continued in verse 7 of that same psalm: "Answer me quickly, O LORD; my spirit faints." At another time he said, "God is our refuge and strength, an ever present help in trouble" (Psalm 46:1).

One of the finest examples for us on how to deal with our sin is found in Psalm 32:5-6:

> Then I acknowledged my sin to you and did not cover up my iniquity. I said, "I will confess my transgressions to the LORD"—and you forgave the guilt of my sin. Therefore let everyone who is godly pray to you while you may be found.

We can do exactly what the psalmist did: Confess the sin of our hearts, and then because we know that God will forgive us, we may exhort everyone in need to pray to the Lord.

A Loving and Understanding Heart Towards Others

When you understand your own depravity, you will identify with others in their struggle against sin. Self-righteous attitudes that are critical and judgmental of others will never minister to broken hearts. A sense of our own sinfulness always makes us more tender in dealing with others.

In Old Testament times, the high priests that God selected were themselves sinful men. The Lord did not send holy angels to perform that office. Why? So that they could "deal gently with those who are ignorant and are going astray, since he himself is subject to weakness" (Hebrews 5:1-3). They offered sacrifices not only for the sins of the people, but for their own sins as well.

Those who delight to walk with God are encouraged in Galatians 6:1-2 to restore those who have fallen into sin, but to do it with "a spirit of gentleness; looking to yourselves, lest you too be tempted" (NASB). In doing this we bear one another's burdens, loving one another, thus fulfilling the law of Christ. A loving heart that bears another's burden flows out of an understanding of personal weakness and susceptibility.

A Willingness to Forgive

Depravity cries out for forgiveness and deliverance. When you think more lightly of your sin than you ought to think, your desire for forgiveness is weak and your capacity to forgive others is small.

Jesus taught Peter a great lesson on forgiveness in Matthew 18:21-35. Peter had asked, "Lord, how many times shall I forgive my brother when he sins against me? Up to seven times?" Peter no doubt thought that seven times was an exceptionally generous number, the maximum a person's love and forgiving spirit could be expected to extend when an offense was continually repeated. But Peter was to be surprised.

Jesus answered him, "I tell you, not seven times, but seventy-seven times." It's like saying there is no limitation upon forgiveness. The parable he used to emphasize his point made it clear that we are all guilty of something, and that we should all therefore be ready to forgive those who wrong us. Our compassion must be rooted in our understanding of human weakness and sin. His concluding words were:

> This is how my heavenly Father will treat each of you unless you forgive your brother from your heart.

Tender-heartedness is crucial when you want to forgive someone who has offended you deeply. We are reminded of that in passages like the following two:

> Be kind and compassionate to one another, forgiving each other, just as in Christ God forgave you (Ephesians 4:32).
>
> Therefore, as God's chosen people, holy and dearly loved, clothe yourselves with compassion, kindness, humility, gentleness and patience. Bear with each other and forgive whatever grievances you may have against one another. Forgive as the Lord forgave you. (Colossians 3:12-13).

Because we have been forgiven so much, so should we forgive others.

Are We Simply a Worm?

Some of you who have been carefully reading this chapter may have a question. Are we simply worms, totally depraved, worthless in every sense, unable to do anything about our condition? Is that the meaning of depravity?

Of course not. The story doesn't end there! That's what the next chapter is all about—keep reading!

1. Karl Menninger, *Whatever Became of Sin?* (New York: Hawthorn Books, 1973), p. 267.

2. Erich Sauer, *The Dawn of World Redemption* (Grand Rapids: Wm. B. Eerdmans Publishing Co., 1951), p. 57.

3. John Owen, *Sin and Temptation* (Portland, Oreg.: Multnomah Press, 1983 reprint), p. 10.

4. Bruce Narramore and Bill Counts, *Guilt and Freedom* (Santa Ana, Ca.: Vision House, 1974), p. 36.

CHAPTER

6

WHAT SHOULD I THINK ABOUT MYSELF?

We live in a world of numbers, credit cards, licenses, checking accounts, telephone and social security numbers, computers—you name it. It's a world of numbers, numbers, NUMBERS! We have arrived (as the book *Megatrends* tells us) at the "Information Age." Information is an enormous business now—we gather information and then try to make some sense of it.

But where does the individual fit into this picture? We want people to use and relate to computers. We assure them that they're "user friendly." We can even program the little boxes to talk to us—but they are still machines. Nothing more.

We live in a highly impersonalized society. The "personal touch" is all but gone. In the midst of a maze of numbers, facts, and organizational machinery, stands the individual, a person created in the image of God—yet who often seems little more than a statistic!

Life can become pretty depressing when you take the time to ponder all of this. Combine the world of numbers with what the Bible says about the sin and depravity of our hearts, and it's hard to find much to get enthusiastic about. Our self-image can plunge to new lows.

Hope dwindles when we are reminded of our sin. It is only restored when we look to the work of Jesus Christ on our behalf and fix our hope on God's salvation, redemption, and promises. Our own self-confidence and self-righteousness can never become the basis of a positive self-image. The Christian view places the work of Christ as the ground for a right conception of self-worth; not the goodness of man.

What Do We Mean by Self-esteem?

Self-esteem or self-worth is a dominant theme in our society and its philosophy about life. The concentration is on personal worth in an effort to establish the importance of the individual.

But is it right?

Is it right to place value upon yourself—to do things for yourself alone, regardless of the effects upon others? Where do altruism, duty, responsibility, and accountability fit in?

Robert Schuller has centered his ministry on self-esteem and has written many books that reflect his commitment to encouraging people to see their value and worth before God. I have many of these books in my library, and you cannot help being impressed with his underlying dedication to self-worth. Much of what he believes is summarized in his book, *Self-esteem: The New Reformation*. He writes,

> I must admit that I am not totally happy with that word, "Self-Esteem." Years ago I tried the word, "Self-Love." I found the pervasiveness of a negative self-image so saturated the minds of persons that most people couldn't handle the term, "Self-Love." I have tried others, "Self-Worth," "Self-Dignity," "Self-Value," "Human Dignity," "Positive Self-Image," "Ego-Needs," "Human Pride," and none are perfect. I can find fault with all words. I have chosen the term "Self-Esteem" simply because I find that it becomes a philosophical bridge on which to build dialogue with other disciplines that deal with the human being: educators, psychologists, criminologists, sociologists. Let me define the term as I use it: Self-esteem is the human hunger for the divine

dignity that God intended to be our emotional
birthright as children created in his image.[1]

That graphically defines what Robert Schuller—who
could be called "the twentieth-century prophet of self-
esteem"—means by the term.

But is this definition correct? Is self-esteem a "human
hunger"? We would probably answer yes; and yet that
seems like a lofty analysis for the sinful desires and corrupt
goals of many among us.

Further, is self-esteem *really* "a human hunger for divine
dignity"? We might wish it to be so, but is it in fact what
people want? If it is, they must not realize it. And then
again, maybe this is wishful thinking, especially in light of
what we've learned about total depravity.

We have to wonder, too, if God really intended that self-
esteem be "our emotional birthright as children created in
his image." That sounds good, but is it true?

How does one know what is true and what is not? The
Christian answers that only God can determine what is
true, and that his views are written down in that wonderful
Book of all books we call the Bible. So then—does the
Bible teach this definition? Robert Schuller and many
others believe that it does.

But others are not so sure. Paul C. Vitz expressed his
doubts about current doctrines of self-worth and self-
esteem in his insightful book, *Psychology As Religion: The Cult
of Self-Worship*:

> Selfist psychology emphasizes the human ca-
> pacity for change to the point of almost totally
> ignoring the idea that life has limits and that
> knowledge of them is the basis of wisdom. For
> selfists there seem to be no acceptable duties,
> denials, inhibitions, or restraints. Instead, there
> are only rights and opportunities for change. An
> overwhelming number of the selfists assume
> that there are no unvarying moral or inter-
> personal relationships, no permanent aspects
> to individuals. All is written in sand by a self in

flux. The tendency to give a green light to any self-defined goal is undoubtedly one of the major appeals of selfism, particularly to young people in a culture in which change has long been seen as intrinsically good.[2]

One of the outstanding statements of Vitz's book is found a few pages later:

From a philosophical perspective, the most obvious difficulty with selfism is that its proponents fail adequately to define or characterize their central concept—the self.[3]

That's why a definition of "*self*-esteem" is so difficult. Placing esteem or worth on someone, I understand. But when you grant yourself that same quality, we must define what we mean. When we do not, we confuse the facts of biblical teaching. The "self" has some serious things wrong with it! How can I place a value on myself? Upon what ground do I exhort myself to do so? Because I have a so-called "right" to do so? Where does that thinking come from? Does the Bible tell me to do so? Is this what God wants me to do—esteem myself as valuable?

A Definition of Self

The word *self* (the root for words like *selfish* or *selfishness*) is described in different ways by different authors and is difficult to discuss because of the way we approach it. To start with, it's a bad word to many Christians; it seems to imply sin. Some deal with it by speaking of the "old self" and the "new self." They insist that Christians have both "selves" working in them at the same time.

If the word *self* means *nature*, then the Christian has two natures, the old and the new (or as some put it, the "carnal" and the "spiritual").

When I asked a Christian friend to describe his true "self," his answer told me a lot. He said, "I have a sinful nature and a new nature from God, the presence of the Holy Spirit within me. Without help from the Holy Spirit, my sinful nature takes control." He went on to say that his "self" has been spoiled by sin so that his mind, emotions, and will were corrupted. He said that his greatest need was to "yield" to his new nature, so that his old nature did not get the upper hand.

Another believer told me, "I'm just a sinner saved by grace." Another said, "A dirty, rotten, depraved sinner who has been forgiven by Christ." One lady said that her "self" is like a caterpillar. It's really a butterfly, but it lives in a caterpillar shell. What interested me about this lady's remark is that she said she wondered whether a butterfly was inside of her, or whether she would become a butterfly when the caterpillar shell was gone. Interesting point!

In Christian terms, I think she was saying something which we all question from time to time. Is my true self a spiritual nature, or is my true self a sinful nature? Am I a butterfly now, or does it mean that I will become one either when I die or when the Lord returns?

Theologians often handle the problem by describing our "position" in Christ. They say our spiritual nature, established by the work of Christ, makes us stand pure before God—that's "positional truth"—but that it is not made full in my experience until the second coming of Christ. Others say that it is made real in my experience as I say no to my sinful self, and say yes to my spiritual self. And some say that the spiritual nature is nothing more than the presence of the Holy Spirit in my life.

The amazing thing about all these definitions of "self" is the reluctance of Christians to think positively about themselves. Most of them equated the "self" with their sinful nature.

The issue of true identity is at stake, and our guide must be the Bible, not our opinions.

The New American Standard Bible has tried to help us by insisting that there is an "old self" (Romans 6:6; Colossians 3:9; Ephesians 4:22) and a "new self" (Ephesians 4:24; Colossians 3:10). The "old self" (or "old man") refers to unbelievers, not believers. The "old self" has been crucified with Christ, and laid aside or put off. It is done for the believer—finished. It's hard to see how a Christian is still an "old self." This "former manner of life" (Ephesians

4:22) is no more. Ephesians 2:1-3 describes this "old self" and leaves no doubt that it refers to unbelievers, not believers:

> And you were dead in your trespasses and sins, in which you formerly walked according to the course of this world, according to the prince of the power of the air, of the spirit that is now working in the sons of disobedience. Among them we too all formerly lived in the lusts of our flesh, indulging the desires of the flesh and of the mind, and were by nature children of wrath, even as the rest (NASB).

So what is the "new self"?

It is described in many wonderful ways in the Bible. In Ephesians 2:10 it tells us that "we are God's workmanship, created in Christ Jesus to do good works." Ephesians 4:24 tells us that the "new self" is "created to be like God" and has been created "in true righteousness and holiness." Colossians 3:10 adds that the "new self" of the believer "is being renewed in knowledge in the image of its Creator." 1 Peter 2:9-10 gives us this marvelous description:

> But you are a chosen people, a royal priesthood, a holy nation, a people belonging to God, that you may declare the praises of him who called you out of darkness into his wonderful light. Once you were not a people, but now you are the people of God; once you had not received mercy, but now you have received mercy.

The Bible frequently calls believers "saints." It tells us in 2 Corinthians 5:17 that "if anyone is in Christ, he is a new creation; the old has gone, the new has come!"

John 3:1-8 describes the spiritual birth of believers. In order to enter the kingdom of God, we must be born again. In verse 6, Jesus said, "Flesh gives birth to flesh, but the Spirit gives birth to spirit." Has that really happened to all believers? Is it true that our essential natures are spiritual, now that we have believed in Jesus Christ as our savior?

WHAT SHOULD I THINK ABOUT MYSELF?

Are we really new creatures in Christ? Is this merely a positional truth, or is it a fact about who we are? Am I a saint only by way of position or standing before God, or am I right now a full-blown, honest-to-goodness saint?

The self represents who I really am. Not my physical body ... not my skills or abilities ... but the real me, my personhood. My true identity is crucial to an understanding of self-esteem or worth. My values are deeply affected by my understanding of who I am and what my possibilities are.

But What About Sin?

One thing is for sure—we all sin. Does that mean that our true identity is identical to what we were before we became Christians? Is our essential nature sinful, and only our standing before God changed?

The apostle Paul wrote about this in Romans 6-8. In chapter 7, he explains the problem of sin. And isn't it fascinating that he separates the sin from the person?

> As it is, it is no longer I myself who do it, but it is
> sin living in me (Romans 7:17).

Lest we think that in ourselves we are no good at all, he says in verse 18, "I know that nothing good lives in me, that is, in my sinful nature." Again, in verse 20, he says, "it is no longer I who do it, but it is sin living in me that does it."

His true self he calls the "inner being" (v. 22), which responds willingly to the law of God. In verse 25 he summarizes by saying, "I myself with my mind am a slave to God's law." Paul's true identity is spiritual, not sinful. Sin *is* present in his mortal body; he does not deny it. In fact, in verse 21 he declared, "I find this law at work: When I want to do good, evil is right there with me."

And what should we make of Paul's statement in chapter 8 that "Those controlled by the sinful nature cannot please God" (v. 8)? Does that refer to a believer or an unbeliever? He must be talking about an unbeliever because of what he said in verse 9:

> You, however, are controlled not by the sinful nature but by the Spirit, if the Spirit of God lives in

you. And if anyone does not have the spirit of Christ, he does not belong to Christ.

It could not be more clear. The believer's true nature is spiritual, not sinful. Sin is present in the body, that's true. And that sin frustrates me. But my essential nature as a Christian is spiritual: I have been born of the Spirit. My spiritual nature does not and cannot sin. First John 3:9-10 makes this quite clear:

> No one who is born of God will continue to sin, because God's seed remains in him; he cannot go on sinning, because he has been born of God. This is how we know who the children of God are and who the children of the devil are: Anyone who does not do what is right is not a child of God; neither is anyone who does not love his brother.

If our theology is correct, the Christian's identity is spiritual, not sinful. I do not want to dispute the unwelcome fact that sin is present in the believer; that would contradict the teaching of 1 John 1:8 and 10, as well as our own experience. But I do want to make it as clear as I can that God has made the Christian a spiritual being, not a sinful one.

What Does All of This Mean?

So what does this mean? It means that our sense of self-esteem and worth is rooted in the redemptive work of Jesus Christ and in the fact that we were born again. Self-esteem for the believer is based on his or her conversion to Christ. That's when our worth was clearly established. I am valuable to God because I am his child (1 John 3:1-2), born of the Spirit (John 3:6) with a spiritual nature that cannot sin (1 John 3:9), a new creature in Christ (2 Corinthians 5:17), the workmanship of God himself (Ephesians 2:10), a saint (Ephesians 1:1; Philippians 1:1), a part of a holy nation and the people of God (1 Peter 2:9-10).

And to all of that, I say a hearty, "Hallelujah, praise the Lord!"

WHAT SHOULD I THINK ABOUT MYSELF?

Any attempt that tries to find esteem and dignity in the unregenerate heart of an unbeliever is limited at best, and deceiving at worst. It is true that everyone has some dignity and worth because of our creation in the image of God (chapter 1). But sin marred that dignity and wrecked that sense of worth and esteem (chapter 5). Self-worth and esteem are restored and made what they could never have been before *only* when we are born again of the Spirit of God and made new creatures in Christ!

No other event in history so clearly establishes our value to God than the death of his Son, Jesus Christ. That was truly God's demonstration of his love for sinful man. We did not deserve it and we did nothing to earn it. Yet our sin was laid on him (Isaiah 53:6). Through Christ's work on the cross, man and woman have been set free from sin, restored to God, and exalted to a high position in Christ, seated with him in the heavenlies (Ephesians 2:6). We are His "workmanship, created in Christ Jesus" (Ephesians 2:10). We are so valuable to God that he ordained the death of his Son, Jesus Christ, to save us.

So Why Do Many Christians Have a Poor Self-image?

If everything we've said is true, then why do many believers still think they're worms? That's a good question.

For one thing, the failure to understand who we really are can lead to a poor self-image and a sense of failure. We can never measure up if we continually see ourselves as rotten—though forgiven—sinners. We are still defeated if we see nothing good or valuable about ourselves.

If we believe that the old self (what we were before we became Christians) is still us, then we will be often defeated. We will still think of ourselves as worms, so horribly depraved and sinful that all hope of victory is lost. Our only escape would be the second coming of Christ, when the sinful nature would be removed. The Rapture then becomes our ticket away from the misery and defeat of this life. What a tragedy that so many believers actually believe this nonsense!

Bill Gothard of the Institute of Basic Youth Conflicts

has some good material on self-acceptance and self-esteem. Many people have been greatly helped by his work. He consistently points out that a person's attitude toward himself greatly influences his attitude toward God, family, friends, future, and a host of other things. He stresses that a negative or poor self-image happens when we let the values and opinions of others influence us rather than what God says about us. How true!

Normally, people tell us things about the outer man rather than the inner man. First Samuel 16:7 says "Man looks at the outward appearance, but the LORD looks at the heart." According to Paul, "outwardly we are wasting away, yet inwardly we are being renewed day by day" (2 Corinthians 4:16). Still, we can be deeply affected by what people say about our outer man.

The problem that most of us with poor self-images have is comparing ourselves with others. We secretly long to be like someone else, either in appearance or ability, and we are not happy with our looks, possessions, job, or success. We can become bitter, resentful, and depressed. It leads sometimes to extreme shyness, withdrawal, or to perfectionism and self-criticism.

People with bad self-images and low self-esteem have trouble loving others and are frequently rebellious. They can't develop close and intimate friendships with people and are often judgmental or self-righteous.

We must guard against getting too simplistic about the emotional problems which cause people to question their worth. But it seems to me that several basic issues need to be addressed.

1. *Unbelief.* Lack of faith and trust in God appears in many forms. Sometimes we simply don't believe what God says about us. We can't accept that we're valuable and have great worth as his children and his treasure. Maybe our families or past experiences have made us feel unworthy, incapable, or inadequate.

But feelings are not facts! If you never received the approval of your parents or you felt that you could never please them, you probably have a bad self-image. But whose opinion is more important, your parents' or God's? God says you are of infinite value! Do you believe that? If not, it is really unbelief that is your problem, not your past experiences.

We don't have to be chained to our background! While it has significant influence on us, praise God that his Holy Spirit can bring us to a proper understanding about ourselves through his marvelous Word, the Bible! His Word can give us the faith and trust in God that may be lacking.

The problems of unbelief can also be severe for those who have been hurt by trusting someone who eventually betrayed them. If someone has disappointed you by letting you down or not keeping a promise, that can hurt. You may find it hard to trust God.

But you will find there is only One you can totally trust, and that is God himself. Your self-esteem and worth will be restored when you learn of his faithfulness and his love for you and what he says about you now that you are a Christian. It's tremendously uplifting to your sense of self-esteem!

2. *Pride.* It sounds surprising, but a poor self-image is not the opposite of pride. Pride is often the reason for the bad sense of self-worth. Pride causes someone to make excessive demands upon himself, to try and prove to himself (or to others) how productive he really is. It gives him a vain, false sense of self-worth when he drives himself to performance that would exhaust anyone else. He feels superior because of it, and the root issue is pride of achievement and success.

Pride makes people do terrible things to themselves in order to prove that others are not worthy of them. This awful malady grips our hearts, convincing us that to harm ourselves will bring others to see how very important we were. Some follow this road long enough that it leads them to attempt suicide in the desperate hope that others will see how much they really needed them.

Pride is behind that over-attention some of us give to our appearance. We are insecure, so we go to extremes to convince ourselves and others that we are not as bad as we think we are. It is a plastic attempt—a veneer, covering the real ache of our hearts. We think that if people saw us as we really are, they would reject us. Since everyone seems obsessed with physical beauty, our pride drives us to compete for attention. When our efforts go unrecognized, our depression grows deeper and our pride more wounded.

Once again, we are looking for self-worth and esteem in the wrong places. We must remember this: We are valuable because of what God has done for us. We are new creatures in Christ!

While some of us buy expensive clothes and become experts in high fashion to gain approval, others choose immodest apparel to attract the opposite sex, even though they are not inwardly pleased with their appearance. Immodesty is a hand reaching out for approval and acceptance. It, too, is rooted in pride, a refusal to accept ourselves as God meant us to be.

It is pride that keeps us from relaxing in God's love and in our true spiritual nature. We struggle for attention, popularity, and approval in wrong ways based on wrong reasons. A bad self-image is often revealed by sloppy appearance. Pride sometimes leads us to choose this tactic in order to get attention or to send a message that we are superior to others and therefore do not have to conform. We want to be different and look different—our pride refuses to identify with the mainstream. Drab-looking clothes and dull colors are sometimes used by Christians to exhibit their "holiness" or "spirituality." Pride lurks there, too.

Pride keeps some of us from wearing the right size of clothes. If we have gained some weight, instead of buying clothes to fit, we continue to cram our new supply of body fat into clothes that are too small for us. Pride will not allow us to admit that what we know in our hearts (and in everyone else's eyes) is true.

We are something far more important than the clothes we wear or the cosmetics we use. We are saints, the people of God, with spiritual natures designed to reflect his glory and excellence. Pride keeps many of us from being what God wants us to be. It keeps us from relaxing—we're too busy trying to prove something.

3. *Wrong values.* What do we believe is important in life? Those things that we deem important we call *values.* And wrong values can lead to a bad self-image.

We live in a world of things. But things do not bring happiness. Insecure people who have a bad self-image are often obsessed with possessions. They become compulsive buyers. They establish their worth by the things they have (or don't have). They try to achieve a measure of self-worth by accumulating clothes, cars, houses, and furniture. Yet materialism leads to a poor self-image.

We are not valuable because of what we own. Our worth does not come from the car we drive or the bank account we have. We are valuable because we are children of the King. We are "co-heirs with Christ" (Romans 8:17)!

4. *Sinful practices.* Another very powerful influence on our self-esteem is sinful practice, which is out of character for believers in Christ. Sin *is* present in our bodies, and we have to face it. We can't try to run away from it. But God has given us wonderful resources to deal with it: prayer, the Bible, and the Holy Spirit.

Whenever there is a pattern of sin in our lives, and we are believers, the usual result is a loss of worth and esteem. We sense we are failures, and our continual sinning only makes it plain. We may then question our true relationship to God. We feel guilt—real guilt, not the false variety. We know that we are Christians and that we should not be doing what we are doing.

There is only one thing to do. We need to repent (change our mind and conduct) and seek to clear our conscience by whatever means necessary. Continual sinning only dulls our enthusiasm and deepens our depression.

Many Christians will punish themselves for either past sins or present patterns of disobedience. Some will use greater performance "for the Lord" as a hopeful answer to the depression of their hearts and their deep sense of failure.

It seems to me that sin always leads to depression in the life of the Christian. Why? Because we are doing that which is contrary to our true self—our spiritual nature, created in Jesus Christ, which cannot sin. So a war rages. First Peter 2:11 puts it this way:

> Dear friends, I urge you, as aliens and strangers
> in the world, to abstain from sinful desires,
> which war against your soul.

By the way, please notice that these fleshly lusts or sinful desires are fighting the soul. The implication is that the soul, the "real you" as a believer, is not sinful in itself (although it is affected by sin). The body has certain appetites and needs. These desires are not wrong in themselves; but whenever they seek to violate the plain commands of God's Word, they turn into sin which torments the true self—your spiritual nature in Christ. This leads to defeat and discouragement.

Is There a Way Out?

That's the bad news. But is there a way out? Of course! First, confess your sin. Don't cover it up, justify it, or defend it. Admit it. God is glorified when we are honest before him. He already knows the real truth.

Second, repent. That means to change your mind (and your conduct) about what you were doing. Stop doing it. If you need to seek the forgiveness of some other person or pay back something, then do it. A clean and clear conscience will result.

Third, accept God's forgiveness. He is faithful and righteous. He must forgive you because of the work of his Son, Jesus Christ, who paid for all your sin. His forgiveness and cleansing is complete, not partial. The sin is removed. If you were to ask the Lord, "Is my sin forgiven?" he would answer, "What sin?"

Fourth, start relying on your spiritual resources. Prayer is helpful in combating temptation (Matthew 26:41), and God's Word helps prevent sinful patterns from developing (Psalm 119:9, 11). The Holy Spirit will help you to control your desires (Galatians 5:16).

Fifth, remember who you really are. Don't let the devil or anyone else tell you that your sin proves your real nature is sinful, not spiritual. Don't let your sense of self-worth and esteem get side-tracked. What people say about your outward appearance or performance does not control your worth. Never! What *does* control it is what God has done and said—and only that!

> A theology of self-esteem is rooted in spiritual birth, a new relationship to God, a new nature from God, a new position before God!

1. Robert Schuller, *Self-Esteem: The New Reformation* (Waco: Word Books, 1982), p. 15.

2. Paul C. Vitz, *Psychology As Religion: The Cult of Self-Worship* (Grand Rapids: Wm. B. Eerdmans Publishing Co., 1977), p. 38.

3. Vitz, *Psychology As Religion*, p. 50.

C H A P T E R

7

IS MY
LIFE
SACRED?

Who are we? Were we created by God in his own image? Or are we merely highly developed beasts? Just what do we *really* think about ourselves? What is our true identity, anyway?

How we answer those questions will largely determine our *values*, the worth we attach to ourselves and to the world around us. How we understand human life cannot help shaping those values. It is there we are most vulnerable. It is at that point that our beliefs about God and the origin of all things become clear ... or muddled.

If God created us, we are faced with certain moral obligations. It is different if we believe we are the chance products of a complex evolutionary process lasting millions of years; then we will discount the sanctity of life and emphasize instead the quality of life. And that can have enormous consequences.

The United States Declaration of Independence asserts "that all men ... are endowed by their Creator with certain unalienable rights ... that among these are life, liberty, and the pursuit of happiness." We need to ask ourselves, "Do we really believe that? Do our unalienable rights come from a Creator? Do we have a basic right to life?" There is no issue today which stirs greater emotions and generates greater debate than this—the right to life. What do we really believe?

WHAT DIFFERENCE DOES IT MAKE?

The United States Supreme Court handed down a decision on January 22, 1973, that deeply affected our understanding of human life. That landmark decision not only legalized abortions in this country, but it also implied that a baby in the womb is not a real person at certain stages of its development. What the court did was to declare on its own that life does not begin with conception, and that none of the documents protecting us—the Declaration of Independence, the Bill of Rights, and the Preamble to the United Nations Declaration on Rights of the Child—apply to the unborn child.

Recall the fifth amendment of the Bill of Rights: "Nor shall any person . . . be deprived of life, liberty or property without due process of law."

And the Preamble to the U.N. Declaration says, "The child . . . needs special safeguards and care, including appropriate legal protection, before as well as after birth."

The World Medical Association's *Geneva Declaration* (which updates the Hippocratic Oath) contains this oath in its standards for the world's physicians:

> I solemnly pledge myself to consecrate my life to the service of humanity. I will practice my profession with conscience and dignity; the health of my patient will be my first consideration. I will maintain by all means in my power the honour and noble traditions of the medical profession. I will not permit considerations of religion, nationality, race, party politics, or social standing to intervene between my duty and my patient; I will maintain the utmost respect for human life from the time of conception; even under threat, I will not use my medical knowledge contrary to the laws of humanity. I make these promises solemnly, freely, and upon my honour.

Doctors who take this oath declare that, "I will maintain the utmost respect for human life from the time of conception." Yet thousands of physicians have chosen to ignore this pledge.

IS MY LIFE SACRED?

In an effort to end the holocaust of abortion-on-demand (which has taken over a million lives each year since 1973), Senator Jesse Helms of North Carolina and Representative Robert Dornan of California proposed a Human Life Amendment a few years ago. This constitutional amendment would overturn the Supreme Court decision allowing abortion and would return America to a policy of defending the unborn. Here's what that amendment said: "The paramount right to life is vested in each human being from the moment of fertilization without regard to age, health or condition of dependency."

Dr. Bernard N. Nathanson wrote this much-quoted passage in the New England Journal of Medicine:

> Some time ago . . . I resigned as director of the Center for Reproductive and Sexual Health. The Center had performed 60,000 abortions. . . . I am deeply troubled by my own increasing certainty that I had in fact presided over 60,000 deaths. There is no longer serious doubt in my mind that human life exists within the womb from the very onset of pregnancy.

President Ronald Reagan called the 1973 Supreme Court decision "a tragedy of stunning dimensions." He said that the tide of abortions "stands in sad contrast to our belief that each life is sacred."

In spite of a multitude of attempts to redefine when life begins, physicians across the country (who have the moral courage) have become increasingly vocal in their opposition to abortion-on-demand. More and more are insisting that human life begins at conception.

One of these writes:

> Modern science in the last decade has brought us a spectrum of knowledge about fertilization and early development that we had only guessed at previously in history. We now know that the sperm contributes 50 percent and that the egg contributes 50 percent of the new life. The sperm contains the genetic code of the

father, and has no life or continuing function beyond the sole goal of its existence, that is, fertilization. The ovum contains the genetic code of the mother and is unquestionably part of her body. It has no other function than to be fertilized, and if it is not, it will die.

When, however, at fertilization, the 23 chromosomes from the sperm join 23 chromosomes from the ovum, a new being is created. Never before in the history of the world nor ever again will a being identical to this one exist. This is a unique being, genetically totally different from the body of the father or the mother, independent, programmed from within, moving forward in an ongoing, self-controlled process of maturation, growth, development, and replacement of his or her own dying cells.[1]

The U.S. Surgeon General, Dr. C. Everett Koop, has written:

Abortion, infanticide, and euthanasia stand before us like dominoes; the first to fall has been abortion on demand. It is a grave issue. Nothing like it has separated our society since the days of slavery.

The pro-choice faction says that children who result from rape or incest, or who are defective or deformed really never have lives worthy to be lived. And they lead us to conclude that nearly all abortions are performed in this country to correct one or another of those tragedies.

It simply isn't true. Abortions in the United States for rape, incest, to protect the life of the mother, or to avoid a defective fetus comprise less than five percent of all abortions. The rest are performed just for convenience. And we are talking about one million abortions a year.[2]

The late Dr. Francis A. Schaeffer, along with Dr. Koop, wrote in their book *Whatever Happened to the Human Race?*:

If people are not unique, as made in the image of God, the barrier is gone. . . . Since life is being destroyed before birth, why not tamper with it on the other end? Will a society which has assumed the right to kill infants in the womb—because they are unwanted, imperfect, or merely inconvenient—have difficulty in assuming the right to kill other human beings, especially older adults who are judged unwanted, deemed imperfect physically or mentally, or considered a possible social nuisance?[3]

We need to linger over those words. Under the regime of Adolph Hitler, Germany chose a position on the "quality of human life" over the "sanctity of human life." And there is a crucial difference! Advocates of a "quality of human life" view will eventually see nothing wrong with eliminating those deemed unworthy or unfit to live. Those who believe in the sanctity of life will honor the lives of all and will seek to protect everyone's rights, from conception to death. No one has the right to take a guiltless person's life. That life is sacred because it has been created in the image of God.

Dr. Koop recognized this principle when he went on to write:

Abortion is an atrocity changing the whole thought process of our country. More than a million unborn lives a year cannot be violently terminated without taking its toll on us as a nation.

Like it or not, God makes the imperfect. And you and I as His stewards have no more right to destroy the imperfect than we have the right to destroy the perfect.

If you believe the universe came about by chance, that you and I evolved from primordial ooze, then there is no unique dignity to human life. Why worry about it?

But if you believe that man was created in the image of God and that he has total, unique, specific specialness, then he should be protected to the best of our ability for all of his lifetime.[4]

What Does the Bible Say About Human Life?

The sanctity of human life—there is no more fundamental value. It determines scores of decisions throughout our lives, and it speaks loudly about our understanding of morality and of God. Still, there is no end of contradictory and confusing viewpoints about the sanctity of human life.

But the real question is this: Who is the authority? Who has a right to tell us what is right? Is it left up to each one to decide individually? Is morality debatable? What makes a view right or wrong? How do we know whether our opinions and decisions are good or evil?

Christians turn to the Bible. They rest in its wisdom and accept its principles. And the Bible declares without hesitation that human life is sacred. It says so in several ways.

1. *Human life is created by God.* Genesis 1:27 says simply, "So God created man in his own image, in the image of God he created him; male and female he created them." That's refreshingly clear! God "formed man from the dust of the ground and breathed into his nostrils the breath of life, and man became a living being" (Genesis 2:7). Human life began when God breathed into Adam, whom he had made from the dust of the ground.

Job declared in Job 10:8, "Your hands shaped me and made me." Later he said, "Did not he who made me in the womb make them? Did not the same one form us both within our mothers?" (Job 31:15). That's clear, too: God creates human life in the womb. Job 33:4 adds, "The Spirit of God has made me; the breath of the Almighty gives me life."

The Bible consistently and frequently emphasizes that we are created by God and that he himself forms us in the womb. "This is what the LORD says—your Redeemer, who formed you in the womb," declares Isaiah 44:24.

Spiritual life is described in similar terms to physical life. God creates the new life of those who believe in his Son, Jesus Christ, as their savior and Lord. In 2 Corinthians 5:17, we read: "Therefore, if anyone is in Christ, he is a new creation; the old has gone, the new has come."

Ephesians 2:10 adds, "For we are God's workmanship, created in Christ Jesus to do good works, which God prepared in advance for us to do."

We are *new creatures, created in Christ Jesus*, according to the Bible. God's creative power has given us new life. Our lives, both physically and spiritually, are created by God.

This immediately gives us great dignity, moral responsibility, and a sense of uniqueness. If we are truly the handiwork of God, then any attempt to murder a human life is an attack against the Creator himself who formed and made us in the womb.

Clinton Birst wrote the following in the magazine *Psychology for Living*:

> We see, then, that abortion neither reverences the sacredness of human life nor of the human body. The body, from conception, is the result of God's handiwork. From conception, it reveals His power and glory. Abortion denies God the praise and glory due Him from His own creation. From conception, the human body is endowed with a special dignity. Abortion denies this flesh the uniqueness of its creation as granted by the Creator.
>
> In our society, the snail darter is protected because we recognize the need to protect an endangered species. If this tiny creature's glory is to be protected, how much more the grand dignity and glory of God as revealed in the human body?[5]

2. *Human life begins at conception.* The failure of scholars, scientists, physicians, lawyers, and judges to deal with the facts on this issue is a tragedy. Understanding when life begins is fundamental to our ethics, to our morality, to our self-worth and our dignity.

A headline appearing on May 5, 1981, in the *Los Angeles Herald Examiner* read, "Science's Biggest Question . . . When Does Life Begin?" The accompanying article reported that

"Last week, at the annual meeting of the National Academy of Sciences, some 150 academy members, representing the nation's scientific elite, debated how to respond. They then passed a resolution, almost unanimously, that said such a statement cannot stand up to the scrutiny of science."

And what "statement" did they refer to? A Senate bill introduced into Congress that said, "The Congress finds that present day scientific evidence indicates a significant likelihood that actual human life exists from conception."

Those 150 scientists went on to say that the question was impossible for them to determine. It asks a question "to which science can provide no answer," they said. Deciding when a developing embryo becomes a person "must remain a matter of moral or religious values."

It seems to me the Bible has little trouble deciding the question. Consider some of its statements:

> Genesis 16:11—"You are now with child and you will have a son."
> Psalm 139:13-16—"For you created my inmost being; you knit me together in my mother's womb. I praise you because I am fearfully and wonderfully made; your works are wonderful, I know that full well. My frame was not hidden from you when I was made in the secret place. When I was woven together in the depths of the earth, your eyes saw my unformed body. All the days ordained for me were written in your book before one of them came to be."
> Matthew 1:18—"she was found to be with child through the Holy Spirit."
> Matthew 1:20—"what is conceived in her is from the Holy Spirit."
> Luke 1:31—"You will be with child and give birth to a son."
> Luke 1:35—"the holy one to be born will be called the Son of God."
> Luke 1:36—"is going to have a child."
> Luke 1:41—"the baby leaped in her womb."

Luke 1:42—"blessed is the child you will bear!"

Luke 1:44—"the baby in my womb leaped for joy."

The passages at the end of this list describe the birth of Jesus Christ and John the Baptist. They clearly maintain that life begins at conception, and that the baby in the womb is capable of human emotion——Elizabeth said her son John "leaped in my womb for joy."

King David spoke of this, too. In Psalm 51:5, he said, "Surely I have been a sinner from birth, sinful from the time my mother conceived me." To what was he referring? Did his mother commit sexual sin that resulted in his birth, or is he saying that sin was present from the moment of his conception? I believe the latter is true. Since the Bible teaches that the physical body is not sinful in itself—although it may be used as an instrument for sin—the presence of sin is in the arena of the soul, the personality of man. David is therefore making as clear a statement as he can that the soul exists at the moment of conception.

The Lord once said to Jeremiah, "Before I formed you in the womb I knew you, before you were born I set you apart; I appointed you as a prophet to the nations" (Jeremiah 1:5).

God knew Jeremiah *as a person* before he was formed in the womb. That's a tremendous statement of the presence of human life at the moment of conception. It demonstrates that from conception we are a real person.

That's the point behind the following article published by the group Crusade for Life:

What we must decide is whether it is possible for a body to be alive, not have a soul, and still be human. If the answer is yes then we had better be ready for a time when the pre-born, the terminally ill, the newborn, the handicapped, those conceived in a test tube or any class of people could be declared soulless. The Bible is silent on how to measure which bodies have souls.

> Logic alone is insufficient to demonstrate that the soul may be added after conception. There must be some evidence, and there is none.[6]

Any position that allows for abortion at any time after conception assumes what it cannot prove.

3. *Human life is more valuable than animals or material things.* Evolutionary thought has deeply changed the way we think about life. Are we simply highly developed animals? The Bible says no!

Jesus said in Matthew 6:25-26 that: "Therefore I tell you, do not worry about your life, what you will eat or drink; or about your body, what you will wear. Is not life more important than food, and the body more important than clothes? Look at the birds of the air; they do not sow or reap or store away in barns, and yet your heavenly Father feeds them. Are you not much more valuable than they?"

Jesus asked two questions:

> "Is not life more important than food, and the body more important than clothes?"

and

> "Are you not much more valuable than they?"

The right answer is obvious—*yes*, a thousand times *yes*! Human life is far more valuable than animals or material things. We must be convinced of the worth of human life, we must respect it and show it the dignity it deserves. We have been created by God, and our lives began at conception.

1 Corinthians 15:38-39 establishes the uniqueness of human life: "But God gives it a body as he has determined, and to each kind of seed he gives its own body. All flesh is not the same: Men have one kind of flesh, animals have another, birds another and fish another."

"All flesh is not the same," the apostle wrote. What a simple but sublime truth! We are completely different from animals. God says we are worth much more!

4. *Human life is to be protected.* Our sense of values must

IS MY LIFE SACRED?

extend to our protection of human life. The right to destroy human life belongs only to God and his laws. It is never an individual's right.

Genesis 9:6 gives us the basic principle: "Whoever sheds the blood of man, by man shall his blood be shed; for in the image of God has God made man."

We protect men and women because we believe that God created humankind in the first place. One of the Ten Commandments was "You shall not murder" (Exodus 20:13). God added these words in Exodus 21:12: "Anyone who strikes a man and kills him shall surely be put to death."

The justice and nature of God's law can be seen in Exodus 21:22-23 (NASB): "And if men struggle with each other and strike a woman with child so that she has a miscarriage, yet there is no further injury, he shall surely be fined as the woman's husband may demand of him; and he shall pay as the judges decide. But if there is any further injury, then you shall appoint as a penalty life for life."

Some pro-abortionists have used this passage to claim that the baby in the womb was not treated with equal respect nor given the same protection as a child already born. But this passage teaches exactly the opposite. The assumption that the "miscarriage" resulted in the death of the baby is incorrect. To the contrary, the survival of the baby through this forced delivery is the reason for a mere fine. If further injury took place, the principle is "life for life." What did that mean? If the baby died, the death penalty was to be exacted—because that baby was human, a real person.

Leviticus 24:17 says, "If anyone takes the life of a human being, he must be put to death." If the baby in the womb is a real human being, then there is a serious problem with abortion. The Scriptures would call abortion *murder*—the killing of a human being. And the penalty for that under Old Testament law was death.

God alone has the right to determine who should live and who should die, according to Deuteronomy 32:39: "See now that I myself am He! There is no god besides me. I put

113

to death and I bring to life, I have wounded and I will heal, and no one can deliver from my hand."

Hannah, the mother of Samuel the prophet, prayed this way as recorded in 1 Samuel 2:6: "The LORD brings death and makes alive; he brings down to the grave and raises up."

A king of Israel said concerning a request to cure a Syrian official of leprosy, "Am I God? Can I kill and bring back to life?" (2 Kings 5:7).

Physical suffering or handicap can never be a reason to take another's life. In Exodus 4:11 we learn of God's direct involvement in these cases: "Who gave man his mouth? Who makes him deaf or dumb? Who gives him sight or makes him blind? Is it not I, the LORD?"

Who are we to judge a person with a physical handicap as unfit to live? Job suffered enormously but never lost his confidence in God. In a moment of great anguish, he said: "Keep silent and let me speak; then let come to me what may. Why do I put myself in jeopardy and take my life in my hands? Though he slay me, yet will I hope in him; I will surely defend my ways to his face" Job 13:13-15).

Job had worth and dignity in that moment of his great suffering and anguish. His so-called friends gave him wrong advice. While he continued to reason about the purposes of God, he refused to take matters into his own hands. Here is a passage for all who sometimes feel tempted to take their own life. Suicide assumes a right that belongs to God alone. Job cried out, "Though he slay me, yet will I hope in him." That's why he refused to take his life or put his life in his own hands. And that's why he could declare:

> As surely as God lives, who has denied me justice, the Almighty, who has made me taste bitterness of soul, as long as I have life within me, the breath of God in my nostrils, my lips will not speak wickedness, and my tongue will utter no deceit. I will never admit you are in the right; till I die, I will not deny my integrity. I will maintain my righteousness and never let go of it; my con-

science will not reproach me as long as I live (Job 27:2-6).

As difficult as his days were, Job refused to let go of his integrity or his confidence in the purposes and plan of God. That's what a value system based on the sanctity of human life can mean in a crisis when despair comes and hopelessness seems to crush your life out.

It is not the *quality* of human life that should concern us, but the *sanctity* of that life. We all hope that the quality improves for every human being on earth; but to substitute quality for sanctity has ghastly results and horrifying consequences.

It is not up to us to determine which person ought to live or die. That right belongs to God alone. Every one of us should have a reluctance and a deep-rooted hesitancy in our hearts when confronted with the possibility of taking another person's life.

These are the principles upon which we should build our basic value system:

1. Human life is created by God.
2. Human life begins at conception.
3. Human life is more valuable than animals or material things.
4. Human life is to be protected.

Dr. Carl F. H. Henry, one of the leading evangelical spokesmen today, wrote in his book, *The Christian Mindset in a Secular Society*:

> The present generation's most horrendous injustice lies in its wanton destruction of prenatal human life, an action by which our society shows brazen disrespect for the dignity and worth of the human fetus. The deliberate medical extinction of a million human fetuses a year exceeds the appalling evil of infanticide in pre-Christian paganism and approves a practice that civilizational conscience in all earlier decades considered reprehensible and morally vicious. It

is supremely ironic that a society that declares human rights an absolute priority should retract the right to life of fetal life it engenders.[7]

1. J. C. Willke, *Handbook on Abortion* (Cincinnati: Hayes Publishing Co., 1975), pp. 9-10.

2. C. Everett Koop, "Deception on Demand," *Moody Monthly*, May 1980, p. 24.

3. C. Everett Koop and Francis A. Schaeffer, *Whatever Happened to the Human Race?* (Old Tappan, N. J.: Fleming H. Revell Co., 1979), p. 89.

4. Koop, "Deception on Demand," pp. 27-28.

5. Clinton Birst, "Abortion: Violence Against the Handiwork of God," *Psychology for Living*, October 1982, p. 11.

6. Crusade for Life, unpublished notes.

7. Carl F. H. Henry, *The Christian Mindset in a Secular Society* (Portland, Oreg.: Multnomah Press, 1984), pp. 102-103.

C H A P T E R
8
WHAT DO I DO NOW?

We live in an age of things. We have more than we have ever had before. In some ways, the "more syndrome" dominates our culture. Advertising is geared toward appealing to our desire for more. We become dissatisfied with what we have even while our passions grow for something better which has just been developed. Our technology amazes the gray hair generation. Computers are changing the direction of our lives and how we understand life. All of this influences our values.

This "high tech" has encouraged a hunger for personal worth and value. John Naisbitt, in his book *Megatrends*, writes about this dilemma:

> During both the 1950s and the 1960s, we mass-marketed the products of that industrial era—products whose regimented uniformities mirrored their industrial base. High tech was everywhere—in the factory, at the office, in our communication, transportation, and health care systems and, finally, even in our homes.
>
> But something else was growing alongside the technological invasion. Our response to the high tech all around us was the evolution of a highly personal value system to compensate for the impersonal nature of technology. The result was the new self-help or personal growth movement, which eventually became the human potential movement.[1]

In a classic illustration of this point, Naisbitt writes:

> High-tech dissonance infuriates people. It's even worse when you again use the technology of the telephone to call a warm friend and instead get more technology. "Hi there, I've gone out for a little while . . ." That's why so many improbable messages are left recorded on those machines.[2]

The illustration speaks for itself!

We long for the personal touch, but machines have gotten in the way. Still, we want the technology, for it makes our lives easier. We like to be comfortable and well-off, and that desire makes it all the easier to develop a value system based more on the quality of life than its sanctity. We might object to technological advance because it threatens our comfort; but who, after all, says no to technology when it conflicts with our moral values?

Let's take one example. Recent advances in audio/visual technology are staggering. Home entertainment is big business, and the high-tech age is bringing it to us. But what has it done to our families? What has it done to our need for personal touch? What has it done to our sense of self-worth and esteem? Many families no longer talk to each other. Family members must now have their own TV sets and stereo equipment so they can watch and listen without the nuisance of other family members.

In programming ourselves to serve the rights and desires of the individual, we have lost a sense of our responsibility to (and need for) each other. But does anyone care? That's the heart of the problem, and our ability to care about these things and for each other has been sadly altered by our changing value system.

One commentator, psychologist Earl Wilson, has said:

> The need to belong ranks high among man's basic needs. Without some sense of attachment to others, a man is adrift in a world filled with uncertainty and doubts concerning personal worth. When a person does not feel he or she be-

longs to anyone, that person is a candidate for despair.[3]

Relationships are essential for emotional and psychological health. But we often feel alone even though others are with us. There is something artificial and superficial about many of our relationships. We speak of the weather, sports, business, politics—anything but about how we feel and what we need in our souls. Someone asks, "How are you?" We reply, "Fine." Why bother with the truth? We don't really believe that anyone wants to know; and even if they did, we're sure they wouldn't have the time or concern to help us.

The Prevalence of "Others" in the Bible

The Bible puts great emphasis on the importance of others. The Greek word translated *others* or *one another* is used 100 times, and a companion word another 160 times.

God's laws in the Old Testament often centered on the relationship and importance of others. Leviticus 19:18 tells us "love your neighbor as yourself," a theme repeated in the New Testament (Matthew 22:39; Luke 10:27). Leviticus 19:11 is another example when it insists, "Do not steal. Do not lie. Do not deceive one another." Verses 15-16 of that same chapter remind us to "judge your neighbor fairly," and "Do not do anything that endangers your neighbor's life."

In one sense, God's laws were established to govern our relationships with others so that we would not diminish their importance nor live our lives neglecting or ignoring them.

The Command to Love Others

None of God's commands could ever do more to establish the importance of others than his frequent instruction to love others. In John 13:34-35, Jesus said: "A new commandment I give you: Love one another. As I have loved you, so you must love one another."

Love for one another is a constant theme on Jesus' lips. In John 15:12 he said, "My command is this: Love each other as I have loved you." Verse 17 adds, "This is my command: Love each other." He repeated that often;

apparently he thought it was important.

People are so important that we are commanded to love them as Jesus Christ loved us.

The apostle Paul writes in Romans 13:8, "Let no debt remain outstanding, except the continuing debt to love one another, for he who loves his fellow man has fulfilled the law."

Again, in 1 Thessalonians 4:9, Paul says, "Now about brotherly love we do not need to write to you, for you yourselves have been taught by God to love each other."

The apostle Peter agrees with Paul when he penned these words: "Now that you have purified yourselves by obeying the truth so that you have sincere love for your brothers, love one another deeply, from the heart" (1 Peter 1:22).

Peter emphasizes the intensity of this love relationship with others. We are to do it "deeply, from the heart." There's no room for insincerity.

John, sometimes called "the apostle of love," speaks of this same thing in several of his writings. In 1 John alone we find many exhortations:

> 3:11—"This is the message you heard from the beginning: We should love one another."
>
> 3:23—"And this is his command: to believe in the name of his Son, Jesus Christ, and to love one another as he commanded us."
>
> 4:7—"Dear friends, let us love one another, for love comes from God. Everyone who loves has been born of God and knows God."
>
> 4:11—"Dear friends, since God so loved us, we also ought to love one another."
>
> 4:12—"No one has ever seen God; but if we love each other, God lives in us and his love is made complete in us."
>
> 4:20—"For anyone who does not love his brother, whom he has seen, cannot love God, whom he has not seen."
>
> 4:21—"And he has given us this command: Whoever loves God must also love his brother."

5:1—"everyone who loves the father loves his child as well."

John repeats this great commandment in 2 John 5: "I am not writing you a new command but one we have had from the beginning. I ask that we love one another."

What Does It Mean to Love One Another?

It's easy to say, "love one another." But what does that mean? What does it involve? How do we do it? That's the crucial question. We all interpret love differently. Sometimes what we call love is nothing more than lust. It is self-centered and self-seeking. We may call it love, but it is not. So what is love?

The ancient Greeks used at least four different words for love. We use one word in English to convey the same idea. I love ice cream, my dog, and my wife—but there is a big difference in the way I love each of those items! (I'm in big trouble if there is no difference!) The four words the Greeks used were:

1. *Eros*—physical/sensual love. This word isn't used in the Bible, but the concept of sexual love is there. English words like *erotic* come from this term.

2. *Storge*—family ties. This word is used of animals as well as people, and usually refers to the love of a parent for a child.

3. *Phile*—psychological/social love. *Phile* refers to the love of friendship or companionship and is used both of God and man.

4. *Agape*—spiritual/divine love. The power behind this word comes from God and is produced by his Holy Spirit in our lives. It centers in sacrifice, and it's not selfish. It seeks to give rather than to receive, and is always interested in the well-being of another without thought of personal gain.

We are hungry for agape love because we often feel used, manipulated, and abused. Everyone seems to be in it for himself or herself. Where is the love of God? How will we know it when we find it?

To Love Others Involves Acceptance and Belonging

Others are important when you accept them as they are and seek to include them in your circle of activities and relationships. That's another way of saying "I love you." When you call a friend and say "I want to be with you," you just spoke words of love.

Romans 15:7 says, "Accept one another, then, just as Christ accepted you, in order to bring praise to God." Romans 12:5 reminds us, "so in Christ we who are many form one body, and each member belongs to all the others."

That's love! We sense our relationship to others, that we belong to each other. First John 1:7 says that believers have "fellowship with one another." We share something in common with other believers—our new life in Jesus Christ. It's so sad that few enjoy that bond between Christian friends.

When we look into the eyes of others and sense our relationship to them, fully accepting them and believing that we are members of the same body ... that's love. That's where it starts, and Christians should understand and practice that more than non-Christians.

To Love Others Involves Humility, Honor, and Care

Others are important when you step aside and consider their needs first. That takes sincere humility. First Peter 5:5 tells us to "Clothe yourselves with humility toward one another." Philippians 2:3 puts it this way: "in humility consider others better than yourselves."

That establishes the importance of others quickly. Most of us are not patient when we communicate. We are anxious to tell our stories and explain our needs, but are often unwilling to listen to and meet the needs of others. It takes a measure of humility. And it takes a dose of honor. Honor means that you regard the other person as really important and that you take the time to listen, care, and help. Romans 12:10 says, "Honor one another above yourselves." Romans 13:7 adds that we should "Give everyone what you owe him: . . . if honor, then honor."

Love honors others and seeks ways in which to build them up, not tear them down. When others are important, you care what happens to them, and you care enough to listen and help. First Corinthians 12:25-26 says: "there should be no division in the body, but . . . its parts should have equal concern for each other. If one part suffers, every part suffers with it; if one part is honored, every part rejoices with it."

Care identifies with the other person. If they are sad, you feel it. If they are excited and happy, you are excited and happy. That's love, and it demonstrates the importance that others have in your life.

To Love Others Involves Forbearance and Forgiveness

Forbearance means that we put up with people—even offensive and overbearing ones. It means patience, willing to endure the differences we have with others. Ephesians 4:2 (NASB) says we should "[show] forbearance to one another in love," and Colossians 3:13 connects it with forgiveness: "Bear with each other and forgive whatever grievances you may have against one another. Forgive as the Lord forgave you."

One of the quickest ways to find out that others are low in our list of priorities is to be impatient with people—unwilling to listen and not really caring about what they say, feel, or do. That hurts. The value system of selfish people is rooted in materialism and self-centeredness, not in the importance of others.

What is one of the greatest things you can do to show how much others mean to you? When you forgive them for something hurtful they have said or done. That's a mark of maturity as well! Many of us are unwilling to forgive because others hardly seem important. Those dominated by selfish interests and personal preferences find no time to accept or forgive others. Why bother, unless others are really important to us?

To Love Others Calls for Encouragement

Encouragement—we all need it. It's a special word, filled with love and the desire to help others. What a joy to be around people who know how to do it!

An introductory remark in a book by Dr. Gene A. Getz

said, "Christians cannot grow spiritually as they ought to in isolation from one another."[4] We need to be supporting each other in love and prayer. One way to demonstrate our concern is by encouraging one another.

If others are important to you, encouragement becomes a necessity. You can't help it . . . you must encourage . . . it flows out of the love you have for others!

Dr. Charles Swindoll wrote in one of his books:

> Will you allow me, in this closing, private chat with you, to pick out one unlovely characteristic frequently found in Christian circles . . . and develop it from a positive point of view? I'm thinking of the lack of encouragement in our relationship with others. It's almost an epidemic!
>
> To illustrate this point, when did you last encourage someone else? I firmly believe that an individual is never more Christ-like than when full of compassion for those who are down, needy, discouraged, or forgotten. How terribly essential is our commitment to encouragement![5]

The Bible considers encouragement enormously important. Just look at some of its reminders:

> I Thessalonians 5:11—"Therefore encourage one another and build each other up, just as in fact you are doing."
>
> I Thessalonians 2:11, 12—"For you know that we dealt with each of you as a father deals with his own children, encouraging, comforting and urging. . . ."
>
> Hebrews 10:24, 25—"And let us consider how we may spur one another on toward love and good deeds. Let us not give up meeting together, as some are in the habit of doing, but let us encourage one another—and all the more as you see the Day approaching."
>
> Romans 1:11, 12—"I long to see you so that I may impart to you some spiritual gift to make

you strong—that is, that you and I may be mutually encouraged by each other's faith."

To encourage others we must spend time with them
("not give up meeting together"). We must have that as our
motive and as the basis of our desire to be with them ("I
long to see you . . . that you and I may be mutually encouraged"). We ought to encourage each other as "a father deals
with his own children" (1 Thessalonians 2:11).

To Love Others Involves Confrontation and Warning

Love is not just encouragement, however. Sometimes
our lack of concern for others is revealed by our failure to
confront and warn loved ones when it is obvious that they
are believing, saying, or doing wrong. Romans 15:14 speaks
of believers who are "able also to admonish one another"
(NASB). Admonishment is warning—confrontation about
beliefs and practices that God says are wrong. You care as a
parent cares who steers his or her child away from a ruined
future caused by wrongdoing in the present.

Galatians 6:1-2 describes this kind of love: "Brothers, if
someone is caught in a sin, you who are spiritual should
restore him gently. But watch yourself, or you also may be
tempted. Carry each other's burdens, and in this way you
will fulfill the law of Christ."

The "law of Christ" is the law of loving one another. It
means bearing one another's burdens by confronting each
other when necessary. The motive is *always* restoration—
not judgmentalism.

Paul told the leaders of the church in Ephesus that a
key to his ministry among them was "to admonish each
one with tears" (Acts 20:31 NASB). Behind the confrontation was a sympathetic heart. Proverbs 27:5-6 gives this advice: "Better is open rebuke than hidden love. The kisses of
an enemy may be profuse, but faithful are the wounds of a
friend."

Sound advice. All the strokes you may receive from an
enemy cannot be compared with one "wound" from a friend
who loves you and who desires to spare you unnecessary
heartache and grief. A friend cares about your reputation

and the effects of sin upon your life. If he loves you and if you are important to him, he will confront you in a loving but firm manner. He doesn't want to embarrass or shame you. Paul wrote in 1 Corinthians 4:14, "I am not writing this to shame you, but to warn you, as my dear children." First Peter 4:8 puts it this way: "Above all, love each other deeply, because love covers over a multitude of sins."

Loving Others

How can we love others? Real love means the following things, at least:

1. Acceptance and belonging
2. Humility, honor, and care
3. Forbearance and forgiveness
4. Encouragement
5. Confrontation and warning

If you love someone, those traits can become second nature. You will find that you sincerely, wholeheartedly, and enthusiastically enjoy showing others that you love them.

But selfish folk will never find time to develop these traits. Why? Others are not a priority. They will step on anyone to get their way and will ignore others to further their own interests. They are selfish—their values have been affected by sin and depravity, and they are unwilling to confess and repent of sin and to trust the work of Jesus Christ on the cross.

Christ died for our sins and rose again from the dead to guarantee our own future resurrection and eternal life. His Spirit within us can produce a love for others. He can turn your goals and values around and focus them on others rather than on yourself. It can happen!

In the Sermon on the Mount, Jesus gave what many people have come to call the Golden Rule. In Matthew 7:12, he said: "In everything, do to others what you would have them do to you, for this sums up the Law and the Prophets."

God's Word is summarized by this principle—do to others what you would have them do to you. When our values are in gear, we cannot ignore or neglect others. They become a priority, and life is filled with grand moments to minister to them. From those encounters and blessed relationships we find joy and happiness.

When others are important we will pray for them (James 5:16) and show hospitality to them (1 Peter 4:9). We will refuse to judge others (Romans 14:13). We won't challenge and envy others (Galatians 5:15, 26), lie (Colossians 3:9), slander (James 4:11), or grumble about others (James 5:9). Those attitudes have to go!

When we begin to think as Jesus thought, when we live as Jesus lived, we will find that our relationships with others are too valuable to destroy with careless words and critical attitudes. If we love others, there will be no thoughts of revenge or getting even (1 Thessalonians 5:15). We will forgive, seeking to restore that which has been broken or strained. Slander and gossip will have no place in our hearts (Proverbs 11:12-13; 16:28; 17:9; 24:28; 25:18).

A Summary on Values

Values are rooted in our understanding and beliefs about the origin of all things. If people are created in the image of God, then our values will center on the importance of each person and on the sanctity of human life. If we believe that life is sacred—a gift from God—we will regard others as important. We will seek to be with others and to encourage and build them up.

Our ability to do that is based on our own sense of worth and self-esteem. And we develop that sense through the new birth, by being born again. Because we are new creatures in Christ—God's own workmanship, created in Christ Jesus, saints, joint-heirs with Christ—we are valuable and of special worth to God and to others. Our sin was dealt with by the death of Jesus Christ on the cross. We have been set free and we have a new spiritual nature from God that is capable of ministering to others with the love of God.

What a glorious privilege we have!

127

1. John Naisbitt, *Megatrends* (New York: Warner Books, 1984), pp. 35-36.

2. Naisbitt, *Megatrends*, p. 41.

3. Earl Wilson, *Needing to Belong* (Portland, Oreg.: Multnomah Press, 1984), p. 3.

4. Gene A. Getz, *Encouraging One Another* (Wheaton: Victor Books, 1981), p. 10.

5. Charles R. Swindoll, *Encourage Me* (Portland, Oreg.: Multnomah Press, 1982), p. 81.

PART THREE

WHERE AM I GOING?

In talking with thousands of persons, particularly college students, from every background and religious or irreligious upbringing, this writer found that most people want reassurance about the future. For many of them their hopes, ambitions, and plans are permeated with the subconscious fear that perhaps there will be no future at all for mankind.

Hal Lindsey, *The Late Great Planet Earth*

CHAPTER
9

WHAT
HAPPENS
WHEN I DIE?

Death—the last enemy and the inevitable fact we all must face. There's no running away from it; thousands of us confront it every day, and no one conquers it. Some of us are taken by surprise. We never dreamed that an accident, heart attack, or even a bullet would end all of our dreams, plans, and hopes. We had so much more that we wanted to do and to get out of life.

Some are told early that they will die, and the emotional effect that brings is enormous. How do you live with the certainty of a terminal illness? What do you do when you learn that you have a disease for which there is no cure and which will certainly kill you in a few years, months, weeks, or even days? What an awesome reality you must now deal with! Your ability to relate to the ordinary radically changes. Issues like what to wear or what color to paint the walls or what restaurant to choose for dinner— now they all seem so insignificant and unimportant. There are weightier matters for you to deal with, for death has made an unavoidable appointment with you and circled it in thick, dark black.

Death affects family and friends. It changes their plans, feelings, and hopes. That loved one who dies takes a part of you. A hole remains which no one is able to fill. You are lonely in a way you do not expect—you hurt and long to touch your loved one again.

Death brings all kinds of pain. Children lose parents,

and parents lose children. Scars often remain for years, even for a lifetime. Death is no friend; it shatters our goals and dreams and sometimes destroys our will to live and our desire to enjoy life to the fullest.

What Is Death?

Much has been written about death, but few of us have paused long enough to examine what we are talking about. No one, after all, comes back from the dead to tell us about it, though we hear from time to time about people who claim that their loved ones have returned to talk with them.

Some religious groups claim the ability to communicate with the dead. But most of us simply don't know what death is like. Is there really a long tunnel with a light at the end?

People generally believe one of two things about death:

1. *Death is annihilation.* Some think death is simply non-existence, the end result of physical decay. When you're dead, you're dead—it's the ultimate end of everything—you cease to exist.

It is easy to understand why many people honestly believe this is true. It certainly looks that way. It is a fact that the body does decay, and the Bible talks about that decay. The story of Adam and Eve contains a prediction of what would happen to their bodies as a result of their sin: "By the sweat of your brow you will eat your food until you return to the ground, since from it you were taken; for dust you are and to dust you will return" (Genesis 3:19).

The body is made up of chemical elements found in the ground. When we die, our bodies decompose and return to dust. Morticians can do some amazing things to a corpse in order to make the body appear normal when folks come to the funeral. But we all know the facts, and we can't change them. We are dust, and to dust we return. Just what God said.

Job spoke often of death during his suffering and in discussions with his three friends. The Bible speaks plainly through Job about what appears to be the hopelessness death brings:

Job 7:5-10—"My body is clothed with worms and scabs, my skin is broken and festering. My days are swifter than a weaver's shuttle, and they come to an end without hope. Remember, O God, that my life is but a breath; my eyes will never see happiness again. The eye that now sees me will see me no longer; you will look for me, but I will be no more. As a cloud vanishes and is gone, so he who goes down to the grave does not return. He will never come to his house again; his place will know him no more."

Job 10:18-22—"Why then did you bring me out of the womb? I wish I had died before any eye saw me. If only I had never come into being, or had been carried straight from the womb to the grave! Are not my few days almost over? Turn away from me so I can have a moment's joy before I go to the place of no return, to the land of gloom and deep shadow, to the land of deepest night, of deep shadow and disorder, where even the light is like darkness."

Job 13:28—"So man wastes away like something rotten, like a garment eaten by moths."

Job 14:1, 2—"Man born of woman is of few days and full of trouble. He springs up like a flower and withers away; like a fleeting shadow, he does not endure."

Job 14:7-12—"At least there is hope for a tree: If it is cut down, it will sprout again, and its new shoots will not fail. Its roots may grow old in the ground and its stump die in the soil, yet at the scent of water it will bud and put forth shoots like a plant. But man dies and is laid low; he breathes his last and is no more. As water disappears from the sea or a riverbed becomes parched and dry, so man lies down and does not rise; till the heavens are no more, men will not awake or be roused from their sleep."

Job speaks for all of us—death seems like the end, and

we ask along with Job, "Man expires, and where is he?" Job asked another question that is a key to the dilemma of death: "If a man dies, will he live again?" (Job 14:14). Apart from the Bible's teaching, there is no way to answer that question confidently.

Job himself wondered greatly what would happen to him after he died:

> My days have passed, my plans are shattered, and so are the desires of my heart. These men turn night into day; in the face of darkness they say, "Light is near." If the only home I hope for is the grave, if I spread out my bed in darkness, if I say to corruption, "You are my father," and to the worm, "My mother" or "My sister," where then is my hope? Who can see any hope for me? Will it go down to the gates of death? Will we descend together into the dust? (Job 17:11-16).

Job centered his hope in what came after death. So he asks some penetrating questions: "Where then is my hope? Who can see any hope for me? Will it go down to the gates of death? Will we descend together into the dust?"

Job asks questions that many still ask today. If annihilation is true, there is not much hope to give. We can be thankful, however, that the Bible does not teach annihilation—there really *is* hope, the kind of hope that only God can provide.

2. *Death is the separation of the body from the soul/spirit.* Death, according to the Bible, is not the end of all things. It is an end—an end to our earthly existence as we have known it. But there is more to come!

Job speaks of this in Job 34:14-15: "If it were his intention and he withdrew his spirit and breath, all mankind would perish together and man would return to the dust."

The body goes to the dust, but the spirit to God. Ecclesiastes 12:7 clearly speaks of this separation of body from soul: "the dust returns to the ground it came from, and the spirit returns to God who gave it."

That's pretty clear, isn't it?

King David of Israel had hope beyond the grave when he wrote in Psalm 16:10, "you will not abandon me to the grave, nor will you let your Holy One see decay." And he wrote in Psalm 90:10 that a separation between body and spirit would occur: "The length of our days is seventy years—or eighty, if we have the strength; yet their span is but trouble and sorrow, for they quickly pass, and we fly away."

There will be an end to life as we now know it; but David says when that happens and it is gone, then we will fly away.

The New Testament is even clearer. James 2:26 tells us that "the body without the spirit is dead." That's what happens at physical death; a body with no spirit in it will decompose. Our Lord said, "Do not be afraid of those who kill the body but cannot kill the soul" (Matthew 10:28). Though the body dies, the soul does not—it continues on forever.

Jesus told a story in Luke 16 about a rich man and a poor man, both of whom had died. Both, Jesus said, were conscious after death and able to communicate. Though they had died physically, they continued to live.

An interesting commentary on the state of the dead is found in Matthew 22:23-33. A group of religious leaders, called Sadducees, questioned Jesus about the resurrection of the dead. They denied that it would ever occur. They believed that death was the final enemy and the end of all.

They gave Jesus a hypothetical problem about a man who died, leaving no children. As was often the custom in those days, the man's brother married the woman. The Sadducees said there were seven brothers who eventually married this woman, all of whom died before she did. Their smug question was, "at the resurrection, whose wife will she be of the seven, since all of them were married to her?"

Jesus replied that they were mistaken about two things at least. First, there is no marriage in heaven. Second, they misunderstood who God was. He told them:

> But about the resurrection of the dead—have you not read what God said to you, "I am the God of Abraham, the God of Isaac, and the God of

Jacob"? He is not the God of the dead but of the living (Matthew 22:31-32).

Jesus was quoting from Exodus 3:6 where God told Moses that he was "the God of your father, the God of Abraham, the God of Isaac, and the God of Jacob." The point is that God's relationship to Abraham, Isaac, and Jacob (they died long before the time of Moses) demands that they were alive at the time he spoke to Moses. Why? Because he is the God of the living, not the dead!

The Sadducees were smart enough not to question the facts about the Jewish fathers, Abraham, Isaac, and Jacob. Jesus insisted that no one can say God is the God of Abraham, Isaac, and Jacob unless those men are still alive. God is not the God of the dead, but of the living.

Physical death simply separates the body from the soul and spirit. The soul will continue to exist forever. That goes for unbelievers as well as believers. In graphic language about the wicked dead, Jesus said "their worm does not die" (Mark 9:44, 46, 48), a quote from Isaiah 66:24. Just two verses before that, Isaiah spoke of the righteous living forever: "'As the new heavens and the new earth that I make will endure before me,'" declares the LORD, "'so will your name and descendants endure.'"

Psalm 23:4 says, "Even though I walk through the valley of the shadow of death, I will fear no evil, for you are with me." Then in verse 6, the Psalmist declares "and I will dwell in the house of the LORD forever." The *forever* comes after the "shadow of death."

Death is not the end of all things, but merely the end of our present earthly existence. Death is a new state of existence in which the soul (personality) lives forever.

The Beautiful Side of Death

It's hard to think of death as something beautiful. We normally think of it as ugly, vicious, an unwanted and reprehensible intruder. But there is a sense in which death can be beautiful: "Precious in the sight of the LORD is the death of his saints" (Psalm 116:15).

The death of a believer is precious to God. He has gone

home. An old Christian song says, "This world is not my home, I'm just a-passin' through." Paul wrote that "our citizenship is in heaven" (Philippians 3:20). Second Corinthians 5:8 says, "We are confident, I say, and would prefer to be away from the body and at home with the Lord."

Home is a beautiful word—and the believer's home is not this planet, but heaven, "with the Lord." Death can be precious if you know that you are going home.

Paul described death as gain rather than loss. He spoke of his desire "to depart and be with Christ, which is better by far." He wrote:

> For to me, to live is Christ and to die is gain. If
> I am to go on living in the body, this will mean
> fruitful labor for me. Yet what shall I choose? I do
> not know! I am torn between the two: I desire to
> depart and be with Christ, which is better by far;
> but it is more necessary for you that I remain in
> the body (Philippians 1:21-24).

What a tremendous perspective! He lived his life for others, but his great desire was to be with the Lord in heaven. Death can be a sweet release into the presence of God.

I was called to the bedside of a dear friend who was dying. He had lived a long life, and now in his eighties he was facing the end of his days on earth.

He said to me that day, "David, pray that I die soon."

"Why do you say that?" I asked.

"Because I want to go home," he said. "I'm tired. And I can't wait to see my Savior."

A few days later he died. His testimony and desire remains with me. He did not fear death—death to him was a blessing. He was released from his suffering and pain.

John caught a glimpse of that when he wrote: "Then I heard a voice from heaven say, 'Write: Blessed are the dead who die in the Lord from now on.' 'Yes,' says the Spirit, 'they will rest from their labor, for their deeds will follow them'" (Revelation 14:13).

Blessed are the dead who die in the Lord! That's the beautiful side of death.

The Fear of Death

As a pastor, I have dealt with many folks who were afraid to die. Death is a terrible enemy to them. It obliterates their plans, wrecks their dreams, and ends their hopes. Many people seem in a race with death, fearful that it will overtake them before they've done the things they hoped to do.

The Bible does call death "the last enemy" (1 Corinthians 15:26). But to the believer, death is a conquered enemy and there is no reason to fear. The book of Hebrews says:

> Since the children have flesh and blood, he too shared in their humanity so that by his death he might destroy him who holds the power of death—that is, the devil—and free those who all their lives were held in slavery by their fear of death (Hebrews 2:14-15).

Believers in Jesus Christ have been set free from the fear of death! The death of Jesus Christ for our sins has smashed the power of the devil. He has no more control over us. Our sin and its consequence—death—has been paid for, and Christ's resurrection guarantees our own resurrection, when we will live with him forever. So much for the fear of death!

People die because they are sinners (Romans 6:23). Death is the ultimate price we pay. It is the final enemy. The good news is that Christ died in our place, paying for our sins. He set us free from the fear of death and guarantees that death cannot control us or defeat us. We will live again!

David said in Psalm 34:4, "I sought the LORD, and he answered me; he delivered me from all my fears" (including the fear of death!).

What Is Happening to the Dead Now?

If death merely separates the body and the spirit, where are the dead now? What are they doing?

Those are good questions . . . and ones that generate much debate. The Bible speaks of the dead as *sleeping* .

Many religions picture the dead as though they were in a long coma. Some speak of the soul sleeping, waiting for the resurrection. In many funeral homes there are rooms for family members to be alone with the dead relative's body. Those rooms are called "slumber chambers." The body is nicely arranged in a casket, and through the use of cosmetics it appears almost alive. People have a chance to work out their emotions in such a room. Many of our funerals try to picture the dead as sleeping.

The interesting thing about the Bible's references to the dead is that the word *sleep* is only used of the body as it is placed in the ground. Daniel 12:2 is a prime example: "Multitudes who sleep in the dust of the earth will awake: some to everlasting life, others to shame and everlasting contempt."

The thing in the ground—the body—sleeps. It sleeps, awaiting its future resurrection. The sleep refers to its lifelessness or motionlessness.

Jesus connected physical death with falling asleep in John 11:11. He said to his disciples, "Our friend Lazarus has fallen asleep; but I am going there to wake him up." The disciples thought he meant literal sleep (v. 13). Jesus had to make it plain for them: "Lazarus is dead" (v. 14).

Death only looks like sleep—it is not literal sleep.

The imagery of sleep also pictures a person resting from the toils and labors of this life. Revelation 14:13 speaks of those who die in the Lord as those who "rest from their labor." The trials are over, the struggles are gone. "Falling asleep" is a beautiful way of describing the physical body in the dust of the ground when its many struggles and hardships are ended.

What About the Soul or Spirit?

We have already seen that the Bible says death is a separation of the body from the soul and spirit, and that the soul lives forever. The soul represents the real person, but without a body.

It is possible, of course, that God has some sort of intermediate body which we take on between the time we die and the time when our bodies are resurrected. We do know that the dead can appear as though they have an earthly body and that they can be recognized. Moses and Elijah appeared with Jesus on the Mount of Transfiguration (Matthew 17:3). And all of them talked together.

A classic example is found in the Old Testament story of Saul and the medium of Endor (1 Samuel 28). Some say that Samuel the prophet (who had died) did not really appear in this story, but that Saul was simply hallucinating or being tricked.

That's not very likely, however, when you read the story closely.

1. *The medium was frightened when Samuel did appear.* This seems to imply that she expected something else to happen (or nothing at all). She cried out, "Why have you deceived me? You are Saul!" (v. 12). King Saul had disguised himself, but when the medium saw Samuel she knew that here was something really extraordinary.

2. *The age and clothes of Samuel were noticeable.* When Saul asked her, "What does he look like?" she replied, "An old man wearing a robe is coming up" (standard look of a prophet) (v. 14).

3. *Saul recognized him clearly.* "Then Saul knew it was Samuel, and he bowed down and prostrated himself with his face to the ground" (v. 14). Knowing the character and intentions of Saul, I doubt if he would have responded as he did if he was not sure this was indeed Samuel. A mere hallucination or mirage would not have shaken him so.

4. *Samuel spoke to him.* The dead are able to communicate. We read in verse 15, "Samuel said to Saul, 'Why have you disturbed me by bringing me up?' 'I am in great distress,' Saul said. 'The Philistines are fighting against me, and God has turned away from me. He no longer answers me, either by prophets or by dreams. So I have called on you to tell me what to do.' "

The response Samuel gave to Saul was not what the king wanted to hear—God had torn the kingdom from Saul and given it to David. It sounds an awful lot like the words of Samuel before he died!

Samuel gave Saul further information later on (v. 19),

which only confirmed that the whole thing really happened. A dead man was brought back, appeared in a recognizable body, and spoke clearly and unmistakably.

The New Testament story of the rich man and Lazarus again confirms the ability of the dead to communicate (Luke 16:19-31). But the communication was between the dead, not between the dead and the living. In fact, the desire to have the dead speak with the living was denied.

The rich man in this story wanted Abraham to send someone from the dead to his five brothers in order to warn them about the place of torment. Abraham replied that if they did not believe Moses and the prophets (the word of God), then they would not believe even if someone should rise from the dead.

This story makes clear something of how the dead exist. Some common activities take place:

(1) They see with their eyes (v. 23).
(2) They have fingers and tongues (v. 24).
(3) They talk and hear (v. 25).
(4) They experience pain and torment (vv. 24-25, 28).
(5) They can remember (v. 25).

Although there have been times when the dead have appeared on earth in a recognizable form, the Bible does not teach that the dead have a physical body to use between the time of death and the moment of resurrection (when the Lord comes).

The apostle Paul said in 1 Corinthians 15 (discussed in detail in the next chapter) that there are only two kinds of bodies—the one on earth, and the one received at the resurrection. He said there are heavenly bodies and earthly bodies (v. 40). But couldn't there be several kinds of heavenly bodies, one for the intermediate state, and one for the future when Christ comes? Paul says no.

The heavenly body is the body we get at the resurrection (1 Corinthians 15:42-49). The passage strongly implies that there is no heavenly body given until the resurrection. While God can make some of the dead appear in a body, it is not their normal condition. Even evil spirits (angels) can appear as men (2 Corinthians 11:13-15).

Do the Dead Know What's Happening on Earth?

After I had conducted a funeral service one day, the widow came up to me at the gravesite and said, "Pastor, does my husband see and know what's going on down here?"

The question is asked a great deal. Do dead loved ones know what we are doing? This often affects people when they contemplate remarriage after the death of a spouse: "Does my former husband or wife see what I am doing?"

While I seriously doubt if they would care—in the light of being with Jesus in heaven—it is important to see what the Bible says.

Isaiah 65:17 says: "Behold, I will create new heavens and a new earth. The former things will not be remembered, nor will they come to mind."

While that speaks of the future state of believers, it may also apply logically to those who have died in the Lord. Why would God punish those who have rested from their struggles down here with the remembrance of them and the knowledge of what is happening on earth from day to day? Revelation 21:4 says: "He will wipe every tear from their eyes. There will be no more death or mourning or crying or pain, for the old order of things has passed away."

While this, too, refers to our future eternal state, why wouldn't it apply to those believers who have already died in the Lord and are now in his presence? If the dead are "blessed" (Revelation 14:13), how can that be reconciled with the possibility of bad memories or knowledge of earthly difficulties or trials? It seems better to assume that all bad memories and knowledge of present earthly struggles are removed from the minds of dead believers who are awaiting the resurrection of their physical bodies.

What About the Wicked Dead?

"Don't give me that hell stuff!" So said a man in his forties with whom I was talking one day. He lectured me that hell was invented by religious types to scare people into believing their message. Many people believe that, and in one respect, I wish they were right. I don't want anyone to go to hell. From how the Bible describes the place, I can't imagine anyone wanting someone to go there.

When people swear at each other, they often say, "Go to hell!" probably not realizing what they have said. First, we don't have the authority to send anyone there; and second, once you know what the Bible really says about hell, you might hesitate saying that to someone ever again!

Common sense argues that the righteous and the wicked ought to be separated. What kind of God would we have if everyone wound up in heaven regardless of how they lived their lives or responded to his message? He is a God of love, of course; but he is also a God of holiness and justice. Without his holiness, his love would be meaningless.

Most people who disbelieve the Bible have a natural tendency to deny that a place of judgment for the wicked exists. But it is never our personal beliefs that make something real or imaginary. The real question is, is there such a place called hell? Is there any way to prove it?

What the Bible Says About Hell

The English word *hell* is often used to translate two Greek words: *hades* (which means "unseen"); and *gehenna* (which refers to a valley called Hinnom). The word *gehenna* is simply a term referring to a valley where children were burned with fire in ancient times as sacrifices to Molech, a pagan god (2 Kings 23:10; Jeremiah 7:31). At the time of Jesus, it was a dump, a place where all kinds of trash, garbage, and sometimes bodies of animals were put. A fire was needed most of the time to remove the stench of the place. That's the word Jesus used to describe the final abode of the wicked dead. Not a very pleasant picture.

The word *hades* is used eleven times in the New Testament and always refers to the abode of the dead. In Luke 16:19-31, it is the place of torment where the rich man found himself. The word is used to translate the Hebrew term *Sheol*, which simply means "grave." Sheol/hades, according to Jesus, was separated into two parts: one for the wicked, and one for the righteous (Luke 16). A great chasm lay between the two.

Following the resurrection of Jesus Christ and his ascension into heaven, believers are never again described as going to sheol or hades. When a believer dies, he goes to be with the Lord in heaven (2 Corinthians 5:8).

The Bible also uses the Greek word *tartarus* in 2 Peter 2:4 to describe the abode of wicked angels (cf. Jude 6-7). The words "lake of fire" are used five times in the book of Revelation to describe hell, and on nine occasions the words "bottomless pit" (pit of the abyss) refer to the lower regions where demons are confined (and out of which they can be let loose at times).

Much of this sounds odd and a little weird to the ears of twentieth-century people accustomed to science, computers, and technology. Yet in the midst of all of our technological advances, there is a great deal of religious fanaticism and wild speculation about ultimate reality. Much of what the Bible says about hell has been misrepresented by various occultic and science fiction advocates. Our movies are filled with biblical concepts of hell, though frequently they are twisted and made to look ridiculous. The real question is still, Is there a hell? Sometimes I feel that if there isn't one, there should be!

The Bible says a lot about the final home of the wicked. It is extremely serious—nothing to joke about. We may not interpret all of the imagery precisely, but that does not detract in the least from the terrible reality of its existence. Jesus called it a place of "outer darkness" where there would be "weeping and gnashing of teeth" (Matthew 8:12; 22:13; 25:30).

In Matthew 25:46 we learn that the wicked go into everlasting punishment. Mark 3:29 speaks of eternal sin. Hebrews 6:2 says there is eternal judgment. Second Thessalonians 1:9 calls it eternal destruction. Revelation 19:20 and 20:10 says that the coming world political leader and his cohort, a world religious leader, will be thrown, along with the devil himself, into a lake of fire where they will be tormented day and night forever and ever. And they will not be alone: "If anyone's name was not found written in the book of life, he was thrown into the lake of fire" (Revelation 20:15).

What awesome words—can they be true? Is there such a place? We would be shortsighted and wholly lacking in compassion if we kept silent concerning the possible tragic consequences waiting for those who rebel against the God who made them. If a child was trapped in an upper bedroom of a burning house and we did nothing to help, who would think us loving? How much less loving would we be if we failed to tell others that there is a hell, if in fact hell really does exist!

In Mark 9:43-48 (see also Isaiah 66:24), Jesus said that hell was a place of unquenchable fire where "their worm does not die and the fire is not quenched." In Matthew 18:8 he called it "eternal fire." Revelation 20:15 calls it "the lake of fire." Some say that the fire is merely a symbol. But how does that make it any less terrifying? A symbol is always less in intensity than that which it represents. If this is not literal fire, only God knows how awful it must be!

Death Is the Inevitable Fact We Must Face!

It doesn't do us any good to run away from death. Death is a reality that we all must face sooner or later. The important issue is to settle what you believe about life after death. Is there a heaven and a hell?

As a young boy of six, I heard a message by my pastor, Dr. Louis S. Bauman, on the wrath of God and the place the Bible calls hell. I knew right then—as I know much better today—that I did not want to spend eternity in hell. I asked my mother how I could go to heaven instead of hell, and she pointed me in the right direction—straight to Jesus Christ. She explained to me that Jesus died for my sins and that they were already paid for. He took my place so that I would not have to go to hell. She encouraged me to place my faith in Jesus and to express that simple confession to God.

I prayed as a child and asked Jesus Christ to come into my life to be my Lord and savior. Through the years my faith has been tested often, and I've had many questions. But one thing still stands—I believe with all my heart that Jesus Christ is my only savior from sin, death, and hell. I will be in heaven some day, not because I deserve it or because I have ever done anything to prove that I am worthy (that would be impossible). I will be in heaven one day because I have personally trusted Jesus Christ as my savior and Lord.

There is no greater issue in life. The most important decision you can ever make will determine where you will spend eternity after you die. It is a decision no one else can make for you. *You* must decide.

> Man is destined to die once, and after that to face judgment (Hebrews 9:27).

CHAPTER
10

IS THERE ANY HOPE?

Job was not so different from any of us when he wondered, "If a man dies, will he live again?" (Job 14:14). We believe that everyone, believers and unbelievers alike, will exist forever in one condition or another. While the destiny of each group is radically different—heaven for one and hell for the other—the Bible makes it plain that there is life after death for all of us.

But what about resurrection? Will we have a new body that will not decay or die again? What does the Bible say about this great hope that burns in the hearts of people throughout the world? Is there a great day coming in which all who have died will be resurrected? And what will those future bodies be like?

The Power of Hope

Hope is a marvelous word—it keeps us going when circumstances would dictate despair and discouragement. We hope that tomorrow will be better than today or yesterday. We hope that our children will respect us, that our spouses will love and care more for us, and that life in general will treat us kindly. We need hope to take the next step. Hope sometimes gets us out of bed and causes us to risk.

A beautiful lady despaired over her husband's lack of love. Her self-worth was low in spite of her physical appeal. She needed hope. Could things ever be different? What hope can we offer to someone disillusioned by continual rejection and apathy?

WHERE AM I GOING?

I was called to the hospital to visit a relative of one of our church members. Her father was dying and she wanted me to give him some hope. His cancer was severe and it was obvious that his days were numbered. Before I could introduce myself, he asked, "What hope can you give to someone who knows he is about to die?"

I told him about life after death, about resurrected bodies and living forever in heaven. It all sounded too good to be true. I told him of Jesus Christ and his love. He died for our sins and made it possible for us through faith in his finished work to live forever in heaven with him.

It's almost impossible for me to describe the joy that came over that dying man's face as he prayed and asked Jesus Christ to come into his life and save him. Three days later he died.

First Corinthians 15:19 says, "If only for this life we have hope in Christ, we are to be pitied more than all men." How sad that we would stake our dreams, hopes, and goals on a fleeting fantasy! Hope must be built on solid ground, on objective facts. Any promise must be rooted in the reliability and faithfulness of the one who makes the claim. God is the one who has promised eternal life to those of us who come to him in faith. Can he be trusted? Will he really accomplish what he has said?

Romans 8:18-25 deals with hope—hope that makes our struggles here worthwhile:

> I consider that our present sufferings are not worth comparing with the glory that will be revealed in us. The creation waits in eager expectation for the sons of God to be revealed. For the creation was subjected to frustration, not by its own choice, but by the will of the one who subjected it, in hope that the creation itself will be liberated from its bondage to decay and brought into the glorious freedom of the children of God.
>
> We know that the whole creation has been groaning as in the pains of childbirth right up to the present time. Not only so, but we ourselves, who have the firstfruits of the Spirit, groan in-

wardly as we wait eagerly for our adoption as
sons, the redemption of our bodies. For in this
hope we were saved. But hope that is seen is no
hope at all. Who hopes for what he already has?
But if we hope for what we do not yet have, we
wait for it patiently.

For the Christian, hope is essential. Our salvation is
tied up in it. The hope centers in the "redemption of our
bodies"; in other words, the resurrection. Our hope is
based on what happens after we die.

Hope for Planet Earth

Hope often seems in short supply around planet earth.
Relationships between people can become strained and
harsh. Political ideals clash with each other. Nations dis-
agree and go to war to prove their point. Nuclear
capabilities have become awesome and frightening. A
leader with warped motives could push a button and
within minutes annihilate millions of people. Human life
is cheap to such demigods.

Political leaders must grapple with this human dilemma. Answers do not come easily. The problems of
famine, disease, pollution, and economic instability now
threaten the entire globe. Nations who once sought to iso-
late themselves and ignore the problems of other nations
now find the tactic virtually impossible.

The whole world now touches itself in a way that our
forefathers could not have dreamed. Computers, which
have brought us from an industrialized society into the information age, remind us continually of our relationships
with everyone on the globe. These machines bring us
closer together statistically—but our struggles with one
another continue.

Some see world government and control as the only
hope. Others view it as the ultimate disaster. It makes
sense on paper, especially if we are to achieve economic
stability worldwide. It makes sense *on paper*; but the real
problem lies so deep that even that solution cannot over-
come it. The real problem lies in the human heart.

The depravity of humankind gives us an awful potential for human enslavement and destruction. Who will control things? What human leaders are capable of leadership with compassion and concern for all? Will power and wealth continue to corrupt and distort the high ideals that most of us desire for all the nations of the world?

Some sociologists are excited about the future. In his popular book, *Megatrends*, John Naisbitt writes:

> We are living in the time of the parenthesis, the time between eras. It is as though we have bracketed off the present from both the past and the future, for we are neither here nor there.
>
> But we have not embraced the future either. We have done the human thing: We are clinging to the known past in fear of the unknown future.
>
> Those who are willing to handle the ambiguity of this in-between period and to anticipate the new era will be a quantum leap ahead of those who hold on to the past. The time of the parenthesis is a time of change and questioning. [1]

Later he adds:

> Although the time between eras is uncertain, it is a great and yeasty time, filled with opportunity. If we can learn to make uncertainty our friend, we can achieve much more than in stable eras. In stable eras, everything has a name and everything knows its place, and we can leverage very little. But in the time of the parenthesis we have extraordinary leverage and influence—individually, professionally, and institutionally—if we can only get a clear sense, a clear conception, a clear vision, of the road ahead. My God, what a fantastic time to be alive! [2]

His optimism is encouraging, but I can't help feeling it rests on shaky ground. His hope that "if we can only get a clear sense, a clear conception, a clear vision, of the road ahead" is precisely the problem. We don't know the future, and the past is a discouraging history of man's inability to control his ambitions and desires.

Others share this pessimism of mine over man's ability to shape his world for the welfare of everyone in it. Carl F. H. Henry writes in his excellent book, *The Christian Mindset in a Secular Society*:

> As a nation we have gone far beyond merely the neglect of God's moral principles to a routine violation of them. We have gone even further to outright rejection of those divine principles in the name of modernity. We are writing our own codes of right and wrong; man in place of God ventures to define the true and the good, and does so in the name of personal creativity and selfism. Today our nation is held together more by a network of governmental controls than by a shared consensus of values. Many of our universities have all but turned their backs on the Judaeo-Christian heritage of revealed truth and divine commandments and have forsaken the pursuit of objective values. Are we as a nation encouraging and inviting the cataclysmic disaster that will plunge not only Western culture but all human history into final judgment?[3]

The Bible speaks of our planet's future in a way that most of us refuse to believe. It predicts a holocaust of war, bloodshed, catastrophes, and calls it the judgment of God. Revelation, the last book of the Bible, paints a terrifying and horrible portrait of this world's destiny.

Billy Graham, in his penetrating book *Approaching Hoofbeats*, writes:

> People pick up their morning newspapers, read the headlines and ask, "What is the world coming to?" Let them read John for God's reply. The 1960s were called the decade of activism, the '70s the me decade. The '80s have been called the decade of survival. As we have seen, many experts project that man will not live to

see 2000. Millions of people all over the world are desperate to know what the future holds. There's a phenomenal rise in the sale of crystal balls and ouija boards. People everywhere eagerly study the signs of the zodiac. Spiritual mediums are prospering. Computers are being used on a massive scale to try to predict the future.

But there is only one authoritative book in the world that accurately predicts what is going to happen in the future—and that is the Bible.[4]

The Bible *does* speak of hope, but that hope arrives after the colossal failures and plans of mankind have been exposed and judged. Our refusal to turn to the God who created us is the fundamental reason our planet will one day be destroyed.

The Bible speaks of a new world that is coming. Hope is possible because God will intervene. After the cataclysmic events of Revelation take place and this planet is judged for its rebellion against God, the Bible says that the Messiah will return and that a marvelous kingdom will be established on earth.

Revelation 11:15 says: "The kingdom of the world has become the kingdom of our Lord and of his Christ, and he will reign for ever and ever."

That's the good news for planet earth!

The prophet Isaiah spoke of this same thing more than 2,500 years ago. Isaiah 65:17 says: "Behold, I will create new heavens and a new earth. The former things will not be remembered, nor will they come to mind."

The apostle Peter echoed that message when he wrote:

But the day of the Lord will come like a thief. The heavens will disappear with a roar; the elements will be destroyed by fire, and the earth and everything in it will be laid bare.

Since everything will be destroyed in this way, what kind of people ought you to be? You ought to live holy and godly lives as you look forward to the day of God and speed its coming. That day will bring about the destruction of the heavens by fire, and the elements will melt in the heat. But in keeping with his promise we are looking forward to a new heaven and a new earth, the home of righteousness (2 Peter 3:10-13).

What Will Change When the Messiah Comes?

What difference will it make when the Messiah comes? What will change? In one word—everything!

There can be no hope for the future and for our planet without the Messiah. The Jewish prophets spoke of this man, a king of all kings, who would come from God and rule this world. He would straighten out the mess we have made, and he would set up a kingdom that will endure forever and ever. Think of the changes!

1. *The physical environment will change*! Enough of pollution—the Messiah will purify the environment. Romans 8:21 says "the creation itself will be liberated from its bondage to decay and brought into the glorious freedom of the children of God." Isaiah 65:17 speaks of "new heavens and a new earth." Isaiah 65:25 tells of changes in the animal world, when "the wolf and the lamb will feed together, and the lion will eat straw like the ox."

The prophet Joel wrote:

> In that day the mountains will drip new wine, and the hills will flow with milk; all the ravines of Judah will run with water. A fountain will flow out of the LORD's house and will water the valley of acacias. But Egypt will be desolate, Edom a desert waste, because of violence done to the people of Judah, in whose land they shed innocent blood (Joel 3:18-19).

"Mountains will drip new wine" and "hills will flow with milk"—what a day that will be! Zechariah speaks of the tremendous changes that will come when the Messiah returns: "And it will come about in that day that living waters will flow out of Jerusalem, half of them toward the eastern sea and the other half toward the western sea; it will be in summer as well as in winter.... All the land will be changed" (Zechariah 14:8, 10 NASB).

Think of it! No more smog alerts ... no pollution of atmosphere ... no more poisoned waterways. The utopia which we have been trying to achieve on earth will finally arrive. We have made a mess of things, but the Messiah will change all of that.

2. A *heavenly city will come down to the earth*! The Bible speaks of three heavens: the atmosphere around the earth; the sun, moon, and stars; and the dwelling place of God. This third heaven where God dwells is called many wonderful things in the Bible: "my Father's house"—John 14:2; "the city of the living God"—Hebrews 12:22; "paradise"—2 Corinthians 12:2-4, Revelation 2:7; "Mount Zion"—Hebrews 12:22; "home"—2 Corinthians 5:8; "kingdom"—2 Timothy 4:18; "a holy place"—Hebrews 9:24 NASB; "the Holy City"—Revelation 21:2,10; "The heavenly Jerusalem"—Hebrews 12:22; "The new Jerusalem"—Revelation 3:12; 21:2.

The word for *heaven* in Hebrew appears 457 times in the Old Testament, while the Greek word pops up 309 times in the New Testament. A few other related words are also used.

It seems incredible to some that the Bible should describe a heavenly city, beautiful beyond description, which will come out of the skies and rest on the earth. It sounds like something out of *Close Encounters of the Third Kind*.

People living 4,000 years ago desired this heavenly city (Hebrews 11:13-16). It is still the desire of people today. Christians are encouraged by Jesus Christ himself to place hope in this future city. In John 14:1-3, Jesus said:

> Do not let your hearts be troubled. Trust in God; trust also in me. In my Father's house are many rooms; if it were not so, I would have told you. I am going there to prepare a place for you. And if I go and prepare a place for you, I will come back and take you to be with me that you also may be where I am.

Read those words again! They proclaim hope and a glorious future to all those who put their faith and trust in

Jesus Christ! What a fantastic prospect!

Revelation 21:2 says this wonderful heavenly city will be "coming down out of heaven from God." Revelation 21:24 tells us that "the kings of the earth will bring their splendor into it." That suggests that it will be sitting on the earth. Verse 25 says that its gates shall never be closed.

According to Revelation 21:16-21, the base of the city is square and each side is 1,500 miles long. The city's wall is 72 yards thick (or about 216 feet high, depending on your interpretation of verses 12 and 17). The height of the city is an astounding 1,500 miles, making it a giant pyramid or cube. The wall has twelve beautiful gates, three on each side, all made of jasper (probably like our diamond). The city is made of pure gold, like clear glass. There are twelve foundation stones, three on each side, made out of the precious gems of earth.

Many believe this description is simply a fairy tale or myth that Christians conjured up to give themselves a measure of hope from the grinding problems of the world. Nothing could be further from the truth!

The truth about this heavenly city was given by Old Testament prophets, confirmed by Jesus Christ himself, and described in great detail by the apostles. Christians are Christians because they believe the message of the Bible about Jesus Christ, his death and resurrection, and the great hope he promised—the glorious return of Jesus Christ and the coming of this heavenly city!

If you have ever had the opportunity to encourage someone dying from a terminal illness, you know the importance of hope. A lady dying of cancer said to me at her bedside, "Please read to me about heaven. I want to know more about where I am going when I die." Tears flooded her eyes as I read the words of the Bible about the heavenly city.

This is our hope! Sadly, many of us are too concerned about today to think about tomorrow. It rarely crosses our minds that we could die today and immediately confirm personally what the Bible teaches about eternity—either heaven or hell.

What About the Resurrection of our Body?

The Bible calls the resurrection of our bodies a hope (Romans 8:18-25). One day we will have a new and glorious body, without the limitations of our present bodies. No more sickness, decay, or death. All sorrow will be gone forever. There will be no reason for sadness or crying. Isaiah 25:8 says, "The Sovereign LORD will wipe away the tears from all faces." Isaiah 35:10 adds, "Gladness and joy will overtake them, and sorrow and sighing will flee away." Isaiah 60:20 says, "and your days of sorrow will end."

That brings encouragement and hope! Revelation 7:17 adds, "For the Lamb at the center of the throne will be their shepherd; he will lead them to springs of living water. And God will wipe away every tear from their eyes." What wonderful relief to those who have experienced heartache, suffering, and trials.

Christians believe all this about the resurrection of the body because they believe that the Bible is true and that the resurrection of Jesus Christ from the dead guarantees he will raise our bodies from the dead as well. A lawyer once told me that it was impossible to prove that Jesus Christ rose from the dead. While he wasn't ready for what I told him that day, that criticism simply will not stand intense scrutiny of the evidence. Few facts in history have been so well documented and established as the resurrection of Jesus Christ. There are five lines of proof.

1. *The authority of the Bible.* According to Luke 1:1-4 and Acts 1:1-3, the reports concerning the resurrection were not based on hearsay or imagination, but upon eyewitness accounts. Peter said, "God has raised this Jesus to life, and we are all witnesses of the fact" (Acts 2:32). Lord Lyndhurst (1772-1863 A.D.), one of the greatest legal minds in British history, said that the evidence for the resurrection cannot be refuted. It is there for all to see and examine.

But is the Bible a reliable account of historical facts? Those who have studied ancient history and archaeology are aware that the Bible is the most accurate account of ancient events ever found.

2. *The absence of the body of Jesus from a closely-guarded tomb.*

IS THERE ANY HOPE?

The Romans were extremely anxious to make the tomb of Jesus secure so that no one could steal his body (Matthew 27:62-66). They even set a seal on the stone which covered the entrance to the gravesite.

So the sight was surprising which greeted the women who came to the tomb early the next morning after Jesus was buried. Mark 16:8 says, "Trembling and bewildered, the women went out and fled from the tomb. They said nothing to anyone, because they were afraid." Matthew 28:8 adds, "So the women hurried away from the tomb, afraid yet filled with joy, and ran to tell his disciples."

The amazing thing is that the disciples themselves would not believe the report. Luke says that "they did not believe the women, because their words seemed to them like nonsense" (Luke 24:11).

If the Romans and Jewish leaders of the first century wanted to stop the spread of Christianity, all they would have had to do was to produce the dead body of Jesus. But they couldn't do so, thank God, because Jesus really had arisen!

3. *The attempt by the Sanhedrin to explain what had happened.* Matthew's gospel says this about religious reaction to the resurrection:

> While the women were on their way, some of the guards went into the city and reported to the chief priests everything that had happened. When the chief priests had met with the elders and devised a plan, they gave the soldiers a large sum of money, telling them, "You are to say, 'His disciples came during the night and stole him away while we were asleep." If this report gets to the governor, we will satisfy him and keep you out of trouble." So the soldiers took the money and did as they were instructed. And this story has been widely circulated among the Jews to this very day (Matthew 28:11-15).

It is sad and yet amusing. In any circumstance, the disciples were hardly able to overpower a Roman guard. Still

157

less were they capable of it when: (1) they were discouraged; (2) they had all forsaken Jesus at the time of his suffering and death; (3) they refused to believe the women when they told them that Jesus had risen from the dead. The facts don't add up that the disciples stole the body.

While there is great question over the authenticity of the book, *The Archko Volume* contains a report allegedly written by Caiaphas concerning the resurrection of Jesus. Whatever its true character, the book makes fascinating reading. In the report of Caiaphas (high priest at the time of the crucifixion of Jesus) we find these words:

> From this I am convinced that something transcending the laws of nature took place that morning, that cannot be accounted for upon natural laws, and I find it is useless to try to get any of the soldiers to deny it, for they are so excited that they cannot be reasoned with. I regret that I had the soldiers placed at the tomb, for the very things that they were to prevent they have helped to establish.[5]

4. *The actions of the apostles after the resurrection.* One of the outstanding facts about the resurrection of Jesus Christ is that it radically changed the lives of the apostles. What a difference from "Then all the disciples deserted him and fled" (Matthew 26:56) to "With great power the apostles continued to testify to the resurrection of the Lord Jesus" (Acts 4:33)!

These disciples of Jesus—transformed from beaten and cowering losers to bold and courageous evangelists— turned the world upside down with their preaching and dedication. They were willing (even glad!) to suffer much persecution after the resurrection, though they had wanted nothing to do with Jesus when he went to the cross. Quite a difference! It's the difference that only the resurrection of Christ could make.

5. *The appearances of Jesus Christ after his resurrection.* Jesus was seen after his resurrection for forty days (Acts 1:3). This was no hallucination—people saw him, talked with him,

concludes, "so shall we bear the likeness of the man from heaven."

There is much that we don't know about the future resurrected body promised to believers in Jesus Christ. But what we do know gives us great hope. Second Corinthians 4:16-18 puts it into perspective:

> Therefore we do not lose heart. Though outwardly we are wasting away, yet inwardly we are being renewed day by day. For our light and momentary troubles are achieving for us an eternal glory that far outweighs them all. So we fix our eyes not on what is seen, but on what is unseen. For what is seen is temporary, but what is unseen is eternal.

I have known some dear friends who have suffered with severe physical handicaps. Each has expressed delight over knowing of the resurrected body they will someday enjoy. It is truly the hope of us all! Sometimes it takes a physical deformity or handicap to make us appreciate that hope. The older we get, the more we anticipate the joys of heaven and the prospects of our new bodies.

King David wrote about this in Psalm 16:8-11:

> I have set the LORD always before me. Because he is at my right hand, I will not be shaken. Therefore my heart is glad and my tongue rejoices; my body also will rest secure, because you will not abandon me to the grave, nor will you let your Holy One see decay. You have made known to me the path of life; you will fill me with joy in your presence, with eternal pleasures at your right hand.

What beautiful words of hope and encouragement! David says the hope of the resurrection:

- *Brings stability to our lives*—"I will not be shaken."
- *Gives us cause for joy*—"my heart is glad" and "you will fill me with joy in your presence."

- *Produces peace in our lives*—"my body also will rest secure."
- *Promises life forever in an imperishable body*—"nor will you let your Holy One see decay" and "you will fill me . . . with eternal pleasures at your right hand."

Paul the apostle challenged believers in 1 Corinthians 15:58 to continue growing in their faith because of the resurrection: "Therefore, my dear brothers, stand firm. Let nothing move you. Always give yourselves fully to the work of the Lord, because you know that your labor in the Lord is not in vain."

No matter how difficult today's struggles may be, nor how heavy the load we must bear, the fact is that our toil is not in vain in the Lord. The hope we have in the return of Jesus Christ and the resurrection of our physical bodies to live forever with the Lord will make it all worthwhile. Esther Kerr Rusthoi wrote this beautiful song:

Ofttimes the day seems long,
Our trials hard to bear,
We're tempted to complain,
To murmur and despair;
But Christ will soon appear
To catch His Bride away,
All tears forever over in God's eternal day.
It will be worth it all when we see Jesus,
Life's trials will seem so small when we see
    Christ;
One glimpse of His dear face all sorrow will
    erase,
So bravely run the race till we see Christ.[6]

IS THERE ANY HOPE?

1. John Naisbitt, *Megatrends* (New York: Warner Books, 1984), p. 279.

2. Naisbitt, *Megatrends,* p. 283.

3. Carl F. H. Henry, *The Christian Mindset in a Secular Society* (Portland, Oreg.: Multnomah Press, 1984), p. 149.

4. Billy Graham, *Approaching Hoofbeats: The Four Horsemen of the Apocalypse* (Waco, Tex.: Word Books, 1983), pp. 208-209.

5. *The Archko Volume* (New Canaan, Conn.: Keats Publishing, Inc., 1975), p. 120.

6. Esther Kerr Rusthoi, "When We See Christ," *Great Hymns of the Faith* (Grand Rapids: Zondervan Publishing House, 1970), p. 149.

SUMMARY: A PERSONAL CREED

Who Am I and What Difference Does It Make?
The Nature and Purpose of Human Life:
A Biblical View

I would like to conclude this book with a summary of its message, but in the form of a personalized creed. This is what I believe. You may find it helpful to do something similar.

1. I was created by God, made in his image.

2. I was born with a sinful nature, and I often demonstrate my depravity by disobeying God's laws.

3. I am part of a family, a father and a mother, an institution designed by God himself.

4. I am married and thus responsible for a new family, with children of my own, thus severing my relationship of dependency upon my original family.

5. I am a father, clearly responsible before God to love, teach, and discipline my children.

6. I am deeply affected by my sinful nature, unable to do good that is acceptable to a holy God, unable to understand spiritual truth by myself, and spiritually dead in terms of my relationship to God—all of this being true apart from God's forgiveness and spiritual life.

7. I am not as bad as it is possible for me to become, nor is the desire to do right absent from my thinking, even though my values and priorities fall short of God's plan and will for my life.

8. My depravity has given me a profound sense of humility, a deep realization of my need for a savior, a clear recognition of guilt, a dependency upon God, a loving and understanding heart toward others, and a willingness to forgive.

9. Because of my faith in the person and work of Jesus Christ, I have a new nature, resulting from spiritual birth, making me a saint, the workmanship of God, a part of a holy nation, the people of God, a real child of God, and extremely valuable to him.

10. My life was created by God and began at conception, and is more valuable than animals or material things,

worthy of being protected and honored as sacred to God and valuable to others.

11. Because life is sacred, others are important to me, needing my love, characterized by acceptance, humility, honor, care, forbearance, forgiveness, encouragement, confrontation, and warning.

12. When I die physically, my soul and spirit will be separated from my body, which will decay in the dust of the ground.

13. As a believer in Jesus Christ, I am aware that at the moment of my physical death, my soul and spirit will be with the Lord, awaiting a future day when my body will be resurrected.

14. My faith in Jesus Christ has saved me from spending an eternity in hell, where all unbelievers will experience the judgment of God.

15. My hope lies in the return of Jesus Christ, the coming of a heavenly city to the earth, and the resurrection of my body from the dead, a heavenly body that will never decay and will never die.

> My hope is built on nothing less
> Than Jesus' blood and righteousness;
> I dare not trust the sweetest frame,
> But wholly lean on Jesus' name.
> On Christ, the solid rock, I stand—
> All other ground is sinking sand,
> All other ground is sinking sand.
>   "The Solid Rock," by Edward Mote (1797-1874)

Feb. =
Fulfilling the Dream

Dana Delany

Catherine
    HERRidge

the rich + shameless

silver & smack
        attack

Alex — CSI Miami

Connie — Ed

Billy Boyd

KT

Xmas + New Year =
    David Hock

FRi. 10 Pms
Robbery Homicide
Division

The Courage of
Love —
Vanessa Wms.